ONE TRUE SENTENCE

It was wonderful to walk down the long flights of stairs knowing that I had good luck working. I always worked until I had something done and I always stopped when I knew what was going to happen next. That way I could be sure of going on the next day. But sometimes when I was starting a new story and I could not get it going I would sit in front of the fire and squeeze the peel of the little oranges into the edge of the flame and watch the sputter of blue that they made. I would stand and look out over the roofs of Paris and think, do not worry. You have always written before and you will write now. All you have to do is write one true sentence. Write the truest sentence that you know. So finally I would write one true sentence

ONE TRUE SENTENCE

Writers & Readers on Hemingway's Art

Mark Cirino and
Michael Von Cannon

WITH AN INTRODUCTION BY
Ken Burns and Lynn Novick

GODINE • BOSTON • 2022

Published in 2022 by GODINE
Boston, Massachusetts

Frontispiece: Handwritten holographic manuscript page from *A Moveable
Feast*. Image courtesy of the John F. Kennedy Presidential Library: Ernest
Hemingway Personal Papers, Manuscripts: A Moveable Feast, Box MS24,
"131. Chapter 2. Miss Stein Instructs. Version One. Manuscript." Used with
permission of the Ernest Hemingway Estate.

LIBRARY OF CONGRESS CATALOGING-IN-PUBLICATION DATA
Names: Cirino, Mark, 1971- editor. | Von Cannon, Michael, editor. | Burns, Ken,
  1953- writer of introduction. | Novick, Lynn, writer of introduction.
Title: One true sentence : writers & readers on Hemingway's art / Mark Cirino and
  Michael Von Cannon with an introduction by Ken Burns and Lynn Novick.
Description: Boston : Godine, 2022. | Identifiers: LCCN 2021055645
  (print) | LCCN 2021055646 (ebook) | ISBN 9781567927139 (hardback)
  | ISBN 9781567927146 (ebook) | Subjects: LCSH: Hemingway, Ernest,
  1899-1961--Criticism and interpretation. | Hemingway, Ernest, 1899-1961--Literary
  style. | American literature--20th century--History and criticism. | English
  language--Sentences. | Authors--Interviews. | Classification: LCC PS3515.E37
  Z74855 2022 (print) | LCC PS3515.E37 (ebook) | DDC 813/.52--dc23/eng/20220118
LC record available at https://lccn.loc.gov/2021055645
LC ebook record available at https://lccn.loc.gov/2021055646

First Printing, 2022
Printed in the United States of America

This book is dedicated to the memory of

SCOTT DONALDSON (1928-2020)

CONTENTS

ONE TRUE SENTENCE

ONE STEP CLOSER
TO THE MAN AND HIS WORK

A PREFACE IN CONVERSATION BY

Mark Cirino and Michael Von Cannon

ONE TRUE SENTENCE was inspired by *One True Podcast,* our show about Ernest Hemingway's life, work, and world. In his memoir *A Moveable Feast,* Hemingway recalls how, while living in Paris in the early 1920s and struggling to write fiction, he would remind himself:

> "'All you have to do is write one true sentence. Write the truest sentence that you know.' So finally I would write one true sentence, and then go on from there. It was easy then because there was always one true sentence that I knew or had seen or had heard someone say."

That idea became the credo of our podcast and for the interviews selected here.

In that same spirit of honesty, creativity, and curiosity, we embraced Hemingway's philosophy and asked contributors to *One True Sentence* their choice for Hemingway's truest sentence and why, and then—as Hemingway wrote—we went on from there.

Michael Von Cannon

Mark, we each have different origin stories for this "one true sentence" project. What's yours?

Mark Cirino

I remember I was in a café on the NYU campus, drinking infinite cups of coffee with my great friend, David Fox. Out of nowhere he asked me, "What's the most Hemingwayesque sentence that Hemingway ever wrote?" I'm sure he was teasing me, because it's kind of a ridiculous question, but I thought about it for a long time. Like years. And that idea about Hemingway's one true sentence is now the crux of every introductory lecture I give on Hemingway. So, I never let go of that concept. I always thought it would be a fun way to get to know someone's version of Hemingway, who he is to them.

A few years after that conversation with David, I created and moderated an American Literature Association panel in Boston called "One True Sentence," where I asked this same question. All the presenters chose a sentence and then talked about it. It was great. It was such a fun event that what I wanted to do at the next Hemingway Society conference was just to write in everybody's welcome packet, "Hey, what's your one true sentence?" and then compile the responses. I thought it would be a nice keepsake. That never happened. It was in Kansas City, and there was a power outage in the hotel—with the electricity out, the only thing that was illuminated was the bar.

Von Cannon

This sounds less a memory and more a dream inspired by a Hemingway story!

CIRINO

Right!? So, there were 180 angry, hot Hemingway scholars crammed in a bar. It was literally a drinking game. I asked Kirk Curnutt, one of the contributors to this volume, "What's your one true sentence in Fitzgerald?" He was about to take a drink, and he just said "blue gardens" right into his cup. And that was all he needed to say. What a great answer! I wanted to go around the room and listen to everyone's sentence. It was a fun curiosity, but to me it also really lent a new insight.

What about you, what's your genesis moment? You didn't go to that conference, did you?

VON CANNON

No, but my story does begin in a bar; however, it's less about one true sentence and more about a crazy idea to start a Hemingway podcast. I was at Bar Hemingway, at the Ritz Paris, to interview the head bartender, Colin Field, about the bar's history and the hotel's recent re-opening. The Ritz is such an important stop on the tour of Hemingway's Paris. As you well know, he "liberated" it from the Nazis, and it was the place where, in the 1950s, two large trunks filled with some of his early Paris writings found their way back into his possession, which led him to write *A Moveable Feast.* That interview with Field wasn't a podcast but inspired the idea for it. When you and I started *One True Podcast* about a year later, "true" became such an important word for many, many reasons. I feel like, in every episode, we're in search of truth as fact, emotional authenticity, the right detail, a sound interpretation. As readers will see here, what's exciting is that contributors have not only chosen a wide range of sentences but they also interpret that word "true" from such different angles.

Throughout this project, what do you think we've discovered about Hemingway's style? What does Hemingwayesque actually mean to you?

CIRINO

I know my definition of that word has become more layered. Hemingway has come to be described on the back of his paperback books as a writer of short, terse prose, but what I find really compelling in this book is that you have people like Marc Dudley talking about a long lyrical sentence from *Green Hills of Africa*, challenging the accepted definition of what is Hemingwayesque. If you look—if you really look sentence-by-sentence—a terse, pared down style is not always the best illustration of what makes him who he was.

Everybody has their own Hemingway, and it's been such a privilege to listen to everybody's version of what inspires them about this writer. Because it's something a little bit different and unexpected every time.

VON CANNON

I completely agree. If Hemingwayesque means short sentences, some of the readers and writers in this book talk about long, complex ones. If it means a style that operates through omission and suggestion, we also discuss how his style is brave or revolutionary because that simplicity doesn't always point to something underneath. Honestly, to me, reflecting on this project, Hemingway's style has come to mean care, discipline, the attention to the well-placed word, even to the point where a preposition like "of" or a pronoun like "it" is so carefully chosen that it carries a profound weight in the sentence. That seems to me his rare talent.

CIRINO

Oh, definitely. Absolutely. It's also forced me to think of the word "true" as a bit more slippery than I ever realized.

Von Cannon

And I think it leads to another question: Is every sentence true in Hemingway? Do you think we could cut out every single Hemingway sentence, put them all in a bag, pull one out at random, and be able to convincingly talk about it for fifteen or twenty minutes?

Cirino

That's a great question. I think that would be an interesting challenge. It would be exhausting! But, you know what, I bet if we interview enough Hemingway readers, we will eventually get through every single sentence in Hemingway.

We talked to Mark Ott about "The river was there" from "Big-Two Hearted River" and to Boris Vejdovsky about "It was raining" from "Cat in the Rain," and if you can structure a Hemingway episode around those apparently uneventful sentences, what couldn't you do? So, even if Sherman Alexie says "I grabbed a cup of coffee" is filler or not necessarily a scintillating prose sentence, some of our readers are ready to take up that challenge of finding transcendence in the mundane.

Von Cannon

That's been striking to me. When we started this, I knew we'd have the opening from *A Farewell to Arms*, the ending from *The Sun Also Rises*, maybe some moments from "Big Two-Hearted River." These are sentences that stay with readers long after they've put down the books. They're phenomenal and discussed here in such thoughtful and surprising ways. But we've also had so many different sentences, sentences that you might have never really noticed and that readers of this book get the chance to truly examine on such an atomistic level.

CIRINO

Just when you think you know a story or a novel, you've read it many times, someone will say something and you say, "Is that sentence in there? I didn't realize that." This ability to keep peeling back ... I mean, I live for that.

You know, in the *Hemingway* documentary by Ken Burns and Lynn Novick, there are these moments when they pan slowly through Hemingway's actual words; either they'll animate the words being written, or they'll show them being typed, then crossed out. And that is a visual version of saying, "Let's forget about him wearing that bulky turtleneck sweater and, you know, having a white beard and drinking and brawling and all that stuff." Let's just focus on the words. When you are reading, when you're thinking about literature, how often do you get to spend an extended period of time, as you were just saying, contemplating the absolutely essential aspect of literary art, which is just the words on the page? It's really been a pleasure to do that because of Hemingway, but also an honor to do it, listening to our brilliant contributors talk about their most intimate connections with Hemingway, which is their personal sentence, their private, secret sentence that they love. I couldn't have hoped for anything more when *One True Podcast* got started, and I hope that this book helps every reader, every Hemingway enthusiast or even some skeptics, take one step closer to the man and his work.

Michael, it can be intimidating to approach a literary titan like Hemingway. I know it was important to you that this "one true sentence" concept, this geeky literary dinner party game of ours, would be a nice entrance for everybody, no matter the depth of their experience.

VON CANNON

It can be intimidating. I really wanted to make sure that this book speaks to scholars, writers, and fans as well as to readers who might not know much about Hemingway, but who won't be lost in these pages.

CIRINO

This book aims to heighten everyone's appreciation of Hemingway and of literature. His work is not supposed to be holy scripture, or some untouchable relic from a museum. It should be worked over. It should belong to the reader. Ultimately, the test for this book's usefulness is if it allows readers to approach Hemingway with greater enthusiasm and insight.

VON CANNON

Well, as Hemingway writes about Nick Adams in "The Last Good Country," "He was all ready now and wanted to start." Let the pursuit begin.

HEMINGWAY:
HIS ONE AND ONLY LIFE

AN INTRODUCTION BY

Ken Burns and Lynn Novick

ABOUT THREE QUARTERS of the way through our documentary on
Ernest Hemingway, his fourth wife, Mary, is habitually fed up with him
and writes him a letter criticizing his carelessness with "your one and only
life." It is an arrow to his heart. Hemingway spent his entire life dealing with
this notion of "your one and only life," his betrayal of it for himself, and the
consequences it has for the people who rally around him, his children, wives,
colleagues, and former friends who are betrayed by him. Every time Mary
says "your one and only life," she's speaking directly to his failure and, under-
lying that failure, his extraordinary success.

Hemingway is arguably the greatest writer of the twentieth century, but as
filmmakers you don't want to stop there. That's the superficial, conventional
wisdom that needs to be checked at the door. What interested us is the really
complicated space between the idea of the person—the prison of that conventional wisdom—and the real person, which is of course unknowable. It's
kind of prying open that door and tolerating the contradictions and tolerating
the undertow and getting to know somebody. Hemingway has unattractive

features that perhaps may not commend him to various times, various genera-
tions, various sensibilities and various sensitivities, but the art will out. As you
dig through a lot of the superficial reality of Hemingway's mask—the macho
posturing, the toxic masculinity—you get at something that's a lot more con-
fusing and very accessible to us today.

Americans are now in a moment of reckoning with national myths, trying
to reconcile and understand and dig deeper below the surface of these myths
of national exceptionalism. A lot of things are specific to America, but Hemingway speaks to a universal human truth. He was so painfully aware of the
human condition that none of us get out of here alive and that the existential
and non-existential responses to that fact are the stuff of everything. He was
amazingly frank when he was good. He was really going right at the heart of
what it is to be present in this moment, to be living life fully, and to be aware
of the dark shadow that passes across every human life. The fact that he was
able to produce what he did with that kind of almost tactile awareness of that
mortality in every sentence is so spectacularly interesting.

It's not to say that other writers haven't dealt with it. All writers do, but
Hemingway's spareness makes it so accessible. You're really getting at fundamental human things. It's like haiku. It's like the best of poetry. It's in his short
stories and novels. There's an elegance to Hemingway's prose, but you don't
see all the hard work that went into it. It looks easy, when you see the final
published version. To get there, it's not easy.

There is every mood you can imagine in Hemingway's letters, fiction, and
the nonfiction, all the different voices of Hemingway. When we were casting
the role of Hemingway for our film, we needed someone who could embody a
young man at the beginning of his journey and an old man with nothing left,
and all the different moods in between: love, excitement, meanness, jealousy.
We actually for a moment thought, "Maybe we should have two different
actors, young and old." Then we said, "No, it has to be one person, but it has to

be one person who can make you feel that arc." Jeff Daniels agreed to be the voice of Hemingway, and he did a magnificent job, delivering way above and beyond anything we could have imagined. We remember the moment when Jeff came in to read those lines from *A Moveable Feast* about "one true sentence." And it's ten times more powerful than anything we had ever dreamt was in that phrase. You're hearing new things.

However, we weren't looking to mimic Hemingway's voice, which is really important to understand. Meaning is more important than anything else for us, so it's about how you inhabit the words and how you give space between each word. Hemingway composed on the iceberg principle of suggestion or implication. As filmmakers, we have a phrase we sometimes use: "Say dog, see dog." It means that you are being very literal; that you're saying what you're seeing. The viewer gets kind of tired of that because it's predictable. You know exactly what you're going to see because you've been told. Instead, we're always looking for surprising, poetic equivalents. If we're lucky, then one plus one doesn't equal two, so you—as a viewer—have a chance also to fill in what you know, to make the connections to what we're not showing you.

In capturing Hemingway's genius and his flaws and his complexities, we keep coming back to his work itself. It bears rereading. The great short stories, the great novels, the greatest works that he created all endure. His influence is in the ether. It is everywhere.

You can see it here in *One True Sentence*. This excellent collection brings together scholars, writers, and great readers to reflect on Hemingway's art and influence using his words as inspiration. Each chapter homes in on one true Hemingway sentence, asking questions like, "Who was Hemingway? How did he reflect and react to his times? What was his style? Why does he matter for us, in our time?" This approach reveals the power of Hemingway's iceberg principle, as the dialogue works to unpack the meaning Hemingway often leaves buried, while also exploring the many ways we, as readers and fans, bring our own expectations and wealth of personal reactions to any given story, novel, or even sentence.

As a success and failure, Hemingway lived his one and only life. And throughout his life, he strove to write one true sentence. We can be thankful he succeeded many times over.

VALERIE HEMINGWAY

What is your one true sentence and why?

For me, the sentence from the first paragraph of *A Farewell to Arms* embodies the "one true sentence" criteria: "The trunks of the trees too were dusty and the leaves fell early that year and we saw the troops marching along the road and the dust rising and leaves, stirred by the breeze, falling and the soldiers marching and afterward the road bare and white except for the leaves." "True," in the sense Hemingway uses it, I take to mean "authentic." It comes from the very essence of the writer's being. In the sentence I quote, I find it defines clearly what is meant. It engages all the senses as one reads. It evokes a visual image: dust, leaves, tanks moving, etc. To the ear, the words read like poetry if said aloud. I could make a case for touch and taste if pushed. Hemingway created magic with his writing when he was at his best.

What do you think the "one true sentence" approach meant to Hemingway?

I think that it worked superbly for Hemingway. It was something he developed over a period of time after much trial and error and a constant endeavor to find the best way he could ply his métier. I think it meant everything to him.

He had formulated a way to use his enormous talent to the best advantage, and he was proud to share the experience with his readers, or any young writer who asked his advice on the subject. Everyone has a particular way of doing things. I am always open to suggestions for improvement no matter what the subject. Hemingway's one true sentence refers specifically to creative writing. Although I have dabbled in poetry and fiction, journalism and nonfiction have been my bread and butter, so I have had to deal with many true sentences, not just one.

"True" was a favored word of Ernest's: "true," "truly," "in truth", would occur in his speech on a daily basis. For me, growing up in Catholic Ireland, "one true" invariably was followed by "God." One true God, not one true sentence. A sentence was a sentence, and we were taught well and truly how to put it together and how to use it. In my youth, my literary mentors were James Joyce, William Butler Yeats, Gerard Manley Hopkins, and G. K. Chesterton, among others. I have added quite a few since then. I tend to favor complexity over simplicity, which perhaps comes from having had a multilingual education: Irish and English were learned simultaneously, French and Latin were part of the curriculum from first form up and, later, Spanish was added. Perhaps that is why I might choose, for instance, Vladimir Nabokov over Hemingway for leisure reading. Maybe I missed the boat and should have paid more attention to that one true sentence.

In 1959, you were sent to interview Hemingway, which for many people would have been an awesome, overwhelming assignment. You write in *Running with the Bulls*, "I didn't have the built-in reverence his name evoked for young and old alike. I did not worship at the Hemingway shrine. I think Ernest found this refreshing." Although you had read some of his works ahead of time, you were approaching him very much like you would any other human being and you were able to relate to him on that level.

True. I had turned nineteen the week before I interviewed him. I had read *The Sun Also Rises*, which was called *Fiesta* in the English edition, when I was fifteen or sixteen. But the first time I ever heard the name Hemingway was when I was twelve. I was in a boarding school, and on my twelfth birthday my mother took me out to see the afternoon show of *For Whom the Bell Tolls*. My mother was very strict about all things cultural. Before we went to the movie, I had to memorize the title and author, *For Whom the Bell Tolls* by Ernest Hemingway, not a common name in Ireland.

—

"Hemingway created magic with his writing when he was at his best."

—

In those days, one never thought about the author of a book, only of its contents. Today, we have a great author culture. People will tell me they are fierce Hemingway fans. When I ask what they've read, they give a quizzical look, followed by a typical exchange, "I know everything about Hemingway's life, and I can tell you the titles of his most famous books. Oh, and I might have read a few of the short stories in school." The first time I met him I made no connection between the works and the writer. However, that glorious summer and fall of 1959, while traveling throughout Spain and parts of France with the Hemingway entourage, working at his side by day and playing catch-up reading his *oeuvre* through the night, Hemingway and his creations melded together in a magical sphere and became inseparable.

You present Hemingway as someone who found it refreshing to relate to people who weren't awestruck and yet as someone who never forgot that he was Hemingway. He seems to have expected a certain reaction from people but also enjoyed not getting that reaction.

I think he probably was a bit ambivalent himself about it. He certainly wanted his literature to be recognized, but he didn't want people prying into his private life, and he really tried to draw a line. For instance, when he asked me to work for him, the only restriction was: "If you work for me, you do not write about my life." Ernest always gave you the stick and the carrot, so he added: "but if you do spend time with me, you will learn about writing. You will learn about life in a way that you wouldn't by sitting at home and doing the occasional interview." He told me a lot about his life because a good part of my work was when he would dictate his letters, both business and personal. What was wonderful about Ernest was that he never kept you in the dark, or assumed that you knew a lot of personal information. There was no need for him to do it, but, whomever he was writing to, he would give me the background of that person and how he knew them and what they meant to him and so on. Even transcribing something that he was saying had to be meaningful because, for him, words were meaningful, and I had a great respect for words, too. We had a connection there, and personality really didn't come into it.

Did you find Hemingway's writing habits, even while traveling through Spain, to be disciplined?

Absolutely, but his writing was a very private thing. I never actually saw him write because he did that on his own early in the morning, and then it was put away. It's funny because the person that most people saw was someone sitting and drinking, carousing, having a good time, whereas his writing was his most personal and private time. I don't think he ever wrote around other people. When I knew him, he had to have a sanctuary, a private place where he wrote—the same place, every day. He had all sorts of little superstitions: a pebble in his pocket, a rabbit's foot, an elk's tooth, all sorts of things I was introduced to that you don't expect in the course of work. When he was finished for the day, he put away the writing and didn't discuss it because he felt that the mind should just rest. If you're working on something, especially if it's something creative, it's like putting the stew on to simmer. Then he would take it up the next day, but he never, ever wanted to discuss what he had written until he felt that it was a *fait accompli*.

➤·◄

VALERIE HEMINGWAY is the author of *Running with the Bulls: My Years with the Hemingways*. As a cub reporter in 1959, she was sent on assignment to Madrid to interview Ernest Hemingway, who later offered her a summer job as a secretary. The job extended through 1960. After Hemingway's death in 1961, Mary Hemingway hired her for the massive and massively important task of archiving Hemingway's papers. She worked in publishing and public relations in New York for almost two decades before moving to Montana with her husband Gregory Hemingway, Ernest's youngest son, and their children.

BRIAN TURNER

ONE TRUE SENTENCE FROM
The Old Man and the Sea

What is your one true sentence and why?

Here it is: "Then the fish came alive, with his death in him, and rose high out of the water showing all his great length and width and all his power and his beauty." I was thinking (well, not to be too much of a pun, but you know), when was I hooked by Hemingway? I thought about *The Old Man and the Sea*, and I didn't read it at first. I read it immediately after hearing a Charlton Heston recording. My English teacher in high school played it for us. For part of a week, we would just go to class and sit there and listen to him. I went back these past couple of weeks to listen to that recording, and I think he reads it too fast. He did a poor job of it, but when I was a kid, I was mesmerized by that recording and his voice. Well, I was mesmerized by the story. That's what got me, and I can see now that I'm hung up a little bit on Charlton Heston reading it. The story is one that transcends whoever might be reciting it. After hearing that recording, my English teacher had us read the book and we looked at it more closely. That line, "with his death in him," you know, there's life and death at the same time.

Your anecdote brings up the point that, even though the novella is about an old man, because of its language and brevity it's usually the first of Hemingway's works assigned to young readers. Looking back on that particular sentence—as part of the bigger story of Santiago's persistence—what did it mean to you as a young man?

It kind of circles back to me with my father because at the time, all through childhood, he was an alcoholic. He had this silent battle that was his own. No one could really help him with it. He was out alone on the ocean, in a sense. I didn't really formulate it this way in my mind at the time, but I can see it now looking back. When I was seventeen, he went to the hospital, got treatment, and he never drank again. Then he learned Spanish, taught himself how to type, learned flamenco guitar. He started jumping out of airplanes. He became a black belt in karate.

As he worked his way towards a black belt, which had been a lifelong dream that I knew that he had, my family went to his promotion ceremony. We were gathered around the mat, and there were several stages he had to go through. He had to do these katas or forms. Then, at the end, he had to do some grappling. The problem was he was not a large man. He was a huge man inside, but the problem was he was smaller. The bigger guys that he was grappling with were told to go full speed at him, but he was exhausted and his grappling skills weren't as good as his regular fighting skills. So, he kept not passing that stage. The only way to become a black belt is to pass each stage to get to the end. If you fail a stage, you have to go back to the beginning and start over. It just kept happening over and over. It was like the fish would run out the line, and he just had to fight it and his hands were bleeding and he had to push his feet up against the gunwale, his face smashed into the tuna on the side, made sick with the smell of it. All of us became the same way around the edge of the scene, watching this man in his boat fighting this great fish, this dream he had. At one point—and I know it was the same for my sister—I wanted to jump in and start punching these guys and help him. Of course we couldn't, because it's his boat and it's his fish to reel in.

That's such a beautiful connection. Brian, you're actually the perfect person to talk to about the "one true sentence" idea. Every word of your own poetry, which is often short and compressed, has to carry some particular kind of power or meaning. In your writing, you're always thinking at a fine-grain level about language. In the sentence that you chose from the novella, we get the word "and" four times; we also get "his death," "his power," "his beauty," and "his great length." It seems like a very intricate sentence for what seems to be such a simple book.

I picked it, in part, because it's not the straight declarative sentence but because I think Hemingway knew that this is a moment where there's a breach in time and space. This is the peak of the story, at least one of the peaks, but probably *the* peak. Maybe there's an emotional peak that comes later, but it's because of this. There is a rupture here, where our lives are in the presence of the sublime.

—

"I think Hemingway knew that this is a moment where there's a breach in time and space."

—

I think that's where his sentence structure had to break open a little bit. You see big concept words like "beauty" and "death." You know, those words are throughout the book, here and there, but he uses them very sparingly. He's much more about the line-and-tackle, the gaff, and all the physical stuff of his life and his body, but none of those moments of the sublime. I think that's why it's lyrical; he wants to hold that moment and freeze time, because he needs that fish to hang in the air so that we can see it. Time itself has stopped for a moment because these two great beings are in conversation with each other. They're seeing each other.

In your book *Here, Bullet*, you used a quote from Hemingway's journalism as an epigraph to your opening poem: "This is a strange new kind of war where you learn just as much as you are able to believe." That seems like quite an elliptical quote. What did that idea mean to you as a soldier?

When I first read it, we hadn't entered the combat zone. So, to me it has a ring of wisdom, but I didn't know what that would mean until I got there. Once I was there, I guess it means that at some point a child might throw a hand grenade into a room or an old man might just shake his head in resignation as we pass, or I might hear it over the radio that someone, another soldier, found an infant under an orange tree in February, but it's a dead infant. Then, as we drive down the road, I might see a man and woman walking very slowly and solemnly, the woman with a blanket in her arms, the man with a shovel. The war that I was in started with a signature of the roadside bomb and the suicide bomber. It switched, after I left, to the era of drone warfare. That's where we sort of still are a little bit: the era of distanced attack. The signature of war changes, I suppose, so in a more practical sense, each war has its own kind of signature.

➤·◄

Brian Turner is the director of the MFA program at Sierra Nevada College and the prize-winning author of two books of poetry—*Here, Bullet* and *Phantom Noise*—as well as the war memoir, *My Life as a Foreign Country*. He has also edited several collections, including *The Strangest of Theatres: Poets Writing Across Borders* and *The Kiss: Intimacies from Writers*.

ALEX VERNON

For Whom the Bell Tolls

What is your one true sentence and why?

I'm going to cheat because it's going to be two sentences back-to-back. So, a line basically. And I'm going to be a little bit meta here as well. It's probably because so much of my scholarly life these days is immersed in *For Whom the Bell Tolls*, but the line that I come back to is toward the end of that novel, when Robert Jordan's death is imminent, and he's reflecting on life. He says, "There's no *one* thing that's true. It's all true."

What is it about that line?

I love that line. Some of the first times I taught the novel, I was like, "What a cheeky, silly, throwaway thing to say." But it's not. Robert has just finished a war in which everyone is absolutely sure that their ideology, their political perspective, is right, whether you're a Marxist or a Fascist or whatever. Even though Hemingway supported the Loyalist effort, he gives us this book where there are all these different perspectives. At one point, we even get a horse telling us what it thinks. So, out of all of that, for him to say it's true—Lieutenant Berrendo's Catholicism is true, someone else's atheism is true—there's a lovely human gesture and generosity in that. I think it also has to do with the fact that, as he's lying there on the ground, Robert's thinking about his experiences, about how all human experience is a lived truth.

When Hemingway went to Italy during World War I, it was as a very young man. During the Spanish Civil War and then World War II, he was an adult, a husband, a father. How had his attitude changed from one war to the next?

As for the first war, Hemingway—along with many, many young American men and Americans in general—wanted to participate. He tried to enlist, could not because of his defective eyes, ended up in the Red Cross as many folks did. He was eager, and it was an adventure. It's very much tainted by his youth and his youthfulness and something that he saw in Stephen Crane's *The Red Badge of Courage.* By World War II, there was a part of him that sort of resisted going a little bit. He was a family man. He had three sons, the oldest of whom was of age, and before the war was over would join OSS [Office of Strategic Services] and become a prisoner in a German POW camp for about six months. There's a great line in *Men at War* where Hemingway says, "This introduction is written by a man, who, having three sons to whom he is responsible in some ways for having brought them into this unspeakably balled-up world, does not feel in any way detached or impersonal about the entire present mess we live in. Therefore, be pleased to regard this introduction as absolutely personal rather than impersonal writing." He did feel the war, and he did feel responsible for his children.

I'm fascinated by the way war becomes personal for Hemingway. Was his stance that people took part in war for both political and personal reasons? Or, maybe, that when you're younger, it's personal, but as you get older you become more conscious of the world?

That's interesting. I'm thinking about the moment in *A Farewell to Arms* when the nurse asks Frederic Henry why he's in the war. He says, "I was in Italy" and then adds, "I speak Italian." There is no political commitment there at all. That's a bizarre scene, too, because Frederic Henry is considerably older than Hemingway was when Hemingway was in the war. He's certainly been in the war for a couple of years at that point (from before the U.S. cared enough to enter), whereas Hemingway was in the war for all of a few weeks. There's a weird sort of apolitical feeling for being in the war. Yet, that kind of cynicism that he has, that really is maybe Hemingway's in 1928-29.

Later on, does Hemingway become more cynical or even less political?

In *For Whom the Bell Tolls*, Robert Jordan's motives are political to a degree, but they're also deeply personal. He has a father who killed himself and a grandfather who was a Civil War cavalry hero. Much of his impulse is to be his grandfather, not his father. Even halfway or so through the novel, he says he's done with politics now, but he goes on and does the bridge mission anyway. You have to ask what are his motives once he's quit the politics. And he's a volunteer. He doesn't have to be there. He and Frederic Henry both could just walk away, but he stays. So, then one has to ask if there are deeper, more personal motivations to his staying, since he has no politics anymore.

In addition to his paternal inheritances, he has predicated the depth of his new love on his imminent death—a death that will let him avoid domesticity, by the way, a death that lets his body integrate with the Spanish earth his lover represents. Oh, and he's fully aware that if he shirks his assignment, his own side might execute him. There's that. Why do readers invariably forget that choice bit of realism for the sake of the book's supposed romantic idealism?

In *Men at War*, Hemingway says, "I have seen much war in my lifetime and I hate it profoundly." How can we square that remark with perhaps

the popular conception of Hemingway. Where is Hemingway on the spectrum between pacifistic and bellicose?

I don't have a quick answer to it. On the one hand, when he says that he hates war, I believe him. I do not think that is lip service at all. He feels that disgust for war. On the other hand, he also recognizes its inevitability and its necessity. Some of the people he admired most in the world were people who were good soldiers. He was also a person of his generation. So, at some level, manhood and masculinity were tied to warfare and to bravery and cowardice and all these things. It was the measure of the man in some ways. He tested it, but he was a person who liked physical adventure and who felt that measure of manhood and who understood war's necessity. To talk about it in terms of martial environments, he certainly admired a lot of soldiers and certainly admired a lot of those leaders whom he felt were really supremely competent.

"I think it's complicated. He does hate war, but there's a part of him that it does stimulate a little bit."

However, he bridled at authority. He would have been a horrible soldier! He couldn't stand people telling him what to do. Robert Jordan is off on his own. In France during World War II, Hemingway goes off on his own for a while and recruits some soldiers and sort of plays commander-in-chief, and does some actions that he gets eventually court-martialed for, although he lies and escapes any punishment. So, yeah, I think it's complicated. He does hate war, but there's a part of him that it does stimulate a little bit. In *A Farewell to Arms*, he compares war to a Chicago meat factory. It's butchery. Yet, people still sort of see Hemingway as this very bellicose, glory-seeking kind of figure.

I think that squaring those images is really weird. I'm actually not sure that Hemingway in his own life squared them perfectly.

Hemingway had a particularly high standard for good war writing. What qualified, in his mind, as good war writing?

He tells us not to trust a piece of war writing that's written while the war is still ongoing. In other words, if there's too much going on, it could be just a scream like with Henri Barbusse's *Under Fire,* and screams don't last. It could have an agenda; it could have a whiff of propaganda somehow. You just can't trust it. On the other hand, he says that if you get too far out from the war, then you run the risk of writing the war as you wanted it to have been, as opposed to how it was. I think for Hemingway, when he talks about what it means to write truly (and, to me, he perhaps uses that word "true" a bit much, which is one reason I initially resisted liking that one true sentence from *For Whom the Bell Tolls*), it's not about messages. It's not about meaning. It's about, as close as possible, conveying the experience—the sights, the smells, the terrors; just trying to recreate the subjective experience of what war was about.

➤•◄

ALEX VERNON is M.E. and Ima Graves Peace Distinguished Professor at Hendrix College. He is the author of two memoirs, *Most Succinctly Bred* and *The Eyes of Orion: Five Tank Lieutenants and the Persian Gulf War.* He has also written numerous books of literary criticism on war writing, including *Soldiers Once and Still: Ernest Hemingway, James Salter, and Tim O'Brien* and *Hemingway's Second War: Bearing Witness to the Spanish Civil War.*

MARK SALTER

In *For Whom the Bell Tolls*, Hemingway's main character Robert Jordan says, "The world is a fine place and worth the fighting for and I hate very much to leave it." That sentence and that phrase, "worth the fighting for," have become associated with Senator John McCain. It seems to have been his one true sentence, or at least one of them. How did Senator McCain come to that novel, and what did that particular phrase mean to him?

Well, he was a little kid, I think twelve. They were living in a Northern Virginia suburb of D.C. at the time. His dad was working at the Pentagon probably. He had been out in his yard and he found a four-leaf clover, and he went to run into his father's library to press it in a book. He pulled a book at random off his father's bookshelf, and it fell open when he put the clover in.

He started reading what was on the page. It was the war atrocity scene from *For Whom the Bell Tolls*, when the villagers are all forced over the cliff. That caught his attention, so he read a few pages. Then he went back to the first page and began reading and read the whole novel that day. And that became his favorite book for the rest of his life. He would talk about it all the time, and he would talk about the protagonist, Robert Jordan, as a real person in his life.

It all meant something to him, but what really meant a lot to him was seeing the world realistically and yet not losing hope. So the ending of that novel to John McCain was an almost perfect ending, where Robert Jordan knows he's going to sacrifice his life for this cause. And all it's really going to do is help his friends escape, but that's enough for him.

The phrase therefore meant the things McCain fought for mattered. Human dignity, equal justice, freedom, representative government; they were worth any amount of sacrifice. But the reason that I called my book *The Luckiest Man* is because that's how McCain viewed himself. Up until his death, knowing he had weeks to live, he was still his calm self, the luckiest man you'll ever meet. And it wasn't just because he had had several near brushes with death or anything. It wasn't that he felt he had been redeemed from his own failings, about which he was honest. But he had redeemed himself by sacrificing for others. And by showing courage and sacrifice in service of others, he had compensated for whatever mistakes he made, flaws he had.

As you describe in your book, a different Hemingway work makes an appearance during the 2008 presidential campaign.

Well, it was very late in the campaign. There's sort of a celebrated moment where McCain's doing a town hall in a suburb of the Twin Cities, and some of his supporters were questioning Obama's citizenship, and he corrects them and defends Obama. Prior to that, he had been campaigning in La Crosse, Wisconsin, and we were in a hotel in the afternoon, with nothing to do until we flew to the Twin Cities that night. We were all gathered in his suite. There was McCain and his wife and about four or five aides. And he said, "Let's order some room service." So, I made a joke that referenced the Hemingway story, "The Short Happy Life of Francis Macomber." McCain turned and said, "That's a great story." And then he said, "But it's not 'The Snows of Kilimanjaro.' That's his best story." Then he pulled out his comically overstuffed, beaten-up, leather briefcase that he carried around with him.

There would always be several books in the briefcase, including his big fat paperback volume of Hemingway stories. He pulled it out and he said, "Listen to how this story begins." And he reads out that *National Geographic* description of Kilimanjaro, how no one knows what the leopard was seeking at that altitude, and the dried carcass of the leopard. And he just kept going and he read it all the way through. It took over an hour and by the time he got to the end he had choked himself up and began to cry. And this is very close to the end of the campaign, which he knew he was losing. It was just this very poignant moment.

When I wrote about that scene at the end of the '08 campaign, when McCain reads "The Snows of Kilimanjaro," to my eye it was a story of profound regret. But to McCain, it was a story of aspiration, looking back at the time he had done something hard for someone else. And when the guy is imagining he's flying and seeing the square top of Kilimanjaro, to McCain, it was like this guy had been redeemed by that sacrifice, and that's what the leopard was doing up there. It was looking for its honor at that altitude. That's what made it "worth the fighting for."

To be a fly on the wall at such a moment. It's interesting to know that the short stories had an impact. Part of your job over several books was to draw out information from the Senator. I wonder if he shared Hemingway's iceberg theory credo, or was he readily forthcoming about his experiences?

The hard parts, the bad parts, he'd describe very economically. He wouldn't add much color to it. For instance, I knew somebody had written before about him in those three days when he'd been tortured so severely after refusing to go home. I read somebody had written a history of the POWs in Vietnam and said that he had attempted to hang himself with a shirt by sticking his shirtsleeve through the louvers of a shutter. So, I asked him about it. He said, "Oh, I didn't do it seriously. I just did it to make the Vietnamese think I would do it, so they'd stop beating the shit out of me." But he wouldn't elaborate any further than that. What he would talk about instead was all the fun he had in prison.

—

"The phrase therefore meant the things McCain fought for mattered. Human dignity, equal justice, freedom, representative government; they were worth any amount of sacrifice."

—

There wasn't a lot of fun to be had when he was in solitary. That was the worst. He said he spent two years in chains in solitary, but he was very close to the guy in the cell next door, and they would communicate either through a tap code or by wrapping their shirts around an enamel drinking cup they had, and they could talk through the walls. They would tell all sorts of jokes and funny stories, and he would tell me all about those. They listened to the propaganda broadcast—Hanoi Hannah, they called her—and they would make fun of things that were on the broadcast. He would tell me about that, the funny stuff that happened to him. When he was put in a group cell later in his imprisonment, he taught a class with a POW friend of his called "The History of the World from the Beginning," and then he would do "Saturday Night at the Movies."

He would also tell them Hemingway stories.

But the hard stuff, the torture, he would talk about things that he knew had a novelistic quality to them. Like a Vietnamese guard loosened the ropes he had been tied up in overnight once. He later saw that guard in the courtyard, and he drew a cross in the dirt with his foot. Things like that. He had an eye. He had a writer's eye. But the really hard stuff, he would be pretty sparse about, and his answers were matter-of-fact.

➤·◄

MARK SALTER was a longtime aide and speechwriter for Senator John McCain, becoming chief of staff and senior advisor to the Senator's presidential campaign. He collaborated with Senator McCain on seven books and has written the captivating book, *The Luckiest Man*.

ELIZABETH STROUT

ONE TRUE SENTENCE FROM

"A Clean, Well-Lighted Place"

What is your one true sentence and why?

The sentence is from "A Clean, Well-Lighted Place": "He would lie in the bed and finally, with daylight, he would go to sleep." When I was looking through many of Hemingway's true sentences, that one just sort of hit me. I had, all of a sudden, an understanding of this sentence as being true. It's very simple, typically simple for Hemingway, and straight to the point.

When you say the word "true," or when Hemingway says it, what does that mean? What's a synonym for "true" in this context?

It's taken me forever to understand what a true sentence is because I was very much guided by those words of Hemingway as a very young person. I think that ultimately you know it when you hear it, but you have to study it for a long, long time. So, to break it down is difficult. I think it needs to be true factually; it needs to be true emotionally; it needs to have not one extra word. It just needs to be the truth of that sentence.

That doesn't necessarily mean true to fact, right?

Right, not true to fact, but within the story shape or the book shape, it has to be true to what's actually happening. Somebody can't walk into the kitchen and then walk through the window. I mean, unless it's fantasy. You know what I'm saying. It has to be true on that very basic level. Then, it has to be emotionally true.

In hearing you read the sentence, a couple of things stood out. At the beginning of the sentence, Hemingway writes, "He would lie in the bed." It strikes me that every other writer I know would have written he would "lie in bed." What does that word "the" add to the sentence?

I was thinking about that as I was choosing that sentence. It's very, very interesting, the word "the." It separates the bed from the man. If you had, "He would lie in bed," the man and the bed become all of one thing. This is, "He would lie in the bed," and that keeps him separate because he is separate.

That's excellent. There's that other, prominent feature of the sentence, which is that phrase marked off by commas: "with daylight."

The "finally, with daylight, …" gives a sense of time passing. Just those three words and the commas, they give the sense of that nighttime experience finally going away.

How do these one true sentences apply to your own work? Do they come naturally to you?

I've been writing from a very, very young age, like the age of four, basically. So, I've been thinking about this for years and years and years, and I do think at this point I can get a true sentence down faster than I used to be able to. I have an image of my hand in a box and there are shapes in that box that I have to make sure are right, but I can't look into the box and see them. I just have to feel them with my hand. When the shape falls perfectly, then I realize, okay, that's a true sentence.

—

"It has to be true on that very basic level. Then, it has to be emotionally true."

—

When you consider your own work, and maybe when you're doing a reading, will you say, "Wow, there are about fifteen sentences in there that are just extraordinary" or "That's one of the best sentences I've ever written"? Can you think about your own work with this same sort of a barometer?

Oh, that's so interesting because I almost feel I have so much trouble judging my own work. Like when I'm working on it, I know, "Okay, this actually is right. This feels right. I'm doing it right. Finally. Now I've got it right." Then, when it's published, and I go back and look at it later, it almost doesn't even feel that connected to me in a certain kind of way. When it's published and I read it, I'll have trouble judging it.

One of the things about "A Clean, Well-Lighted Place" is that it's so short. From your perspective, to create this kind of universe that Hemingway does in maybe three pages, what's the challenge?

It's remarkable because, first of all, he doesn't attribute most of the speech. That's an interesting dilemma in a way, except it's not because it all works. As I was reading this story, I all of a sudden saw something that I hadn't noticed before, which is that the narrator is really an interesting narrator. You might think, at first blush, that this story was more or less from the older waiter's point of view, but, in fact, the narrator is further away. He's up there because at the start of this story, "the old man liked to sit late." This is not the waiter. This is the old man in the café: "the old man liked to sit late because he was deaf and now at night it was quiet and he felt the difference." So, we're inside this man's head. Hemingway has given us permission to understand that this man feels the difference, even though he's deaf, between the noisy café and the quiet café, and I thought that was really fascinating because it does open us up to allow us, even for just that one brief moment, to be that deaf man with that one word "felt."

With this story's themes of isolation and old age, it's sometimes hard to remember that Hemingway wrote it when he was in his early thirties. There's a great quote from your book *My Name Is Lucy Barton*: "Lonely was the first flavor I had tasted in my life, and it was always there, hidden inside the crevices of my mouth, reminding me." That is such a beautiful sentence. How is the theme of loneliness woven through your work?

I don't think that it's a conscious thing. All I do when I work is I try to write about the person that I'm writing about as carefully and as truthfully as I can. I try so hard to get inside that character because I've always been character-driven. I'm not driven thematically, is what I'm saying. I don't have an idea. It comes to me in the form of a person, and that person I need to inhabit as fully as I can, using whatever parts of myself that I can attach to this character, because we don't ever really know what it feels like to be another person. When you think about it, it's kind of horrifying. Years ago, when I picked up a book of fiction, I remember thinking, "Oh, I've had that thought." That was when I understood fiction is one way that we can actually understand what it's like to be another person. I think I was hooked from that moment on to just try and always figure out what it feels like to be another person. When I'm writing, I'm just trying to get that person down as honestly as I can. Then I realize, later, that there are themes, of course, to my work, and that loneliness is one of them.

I'm thinking about Hemingway saying in his Nobel Prize speech, "Writing, at its best, is a lonely life."

Yeah, except when the work is going well, there's nothing like it. So, you wait for those moments when you feel like it's actually going well.

People who aren't that invested in the story could read "A Clean, Well-Lighted Place" and wonder what's going on. With Hemingway's notion of the iceberg principle in mind, what is your negotiation between what you tell your readers and what you withhold or suggest?

I want to leave space between the sentences for the reader to enter with their own story. That, to me, is important because everybody will bring their own story to the text, and it will become almost a different story for everybody who reads it. The denser the prose is, or the more details I give that I don't need to give, it's almost like it blocks the reader from being able to enter in.

The sentence that you point out is the third to last sentence in "A Clean, Well-Lighted Place." So, I also want to ask you about the sense of an ending, about the challenge of ending this story, which deals with the contemplation of suicide. The narrator says, "After all, he said to himself, it is probably only insomnia. Many must have it." An ironic ending. What are endings like for you? Do you find that process similar with every project or does it depend on the book?

It depends on what I'm writing. It's funny because I never write anything from beginning to end, even a story. I just don't write from beginning to end. For the last story in *Olive Kitteridge*, I had written that scene way before I even knew that story was going to exist. It was so interesting to me, and I put it aside and wrote "END?" on top. Then months later I realized, okay, here's a story. Then, all of a sudden, I thought, "Wait a minute, I have the end for this story and the end for the book." So, that was weird and interesting. That sometimes happens; that wasn't the only time that's happened. Otherwise, I don't know how it will end until I get there.

>-◄

ELIZABETH STROUT is the Pulitzer Prize-winning author of *Olive Kitteridge* as well as numerous other novels, including *Olive, Again, My Name Is Lucy Barton,* and *Anything Is Possible.*

LESLEY M. M. BLUME

ONE TRUE SENTENCE FROM
The Sun Also Rises

What is your one true sentence and why?

How can you top "Isn't it pretty to think so?"? It kills me. Hemingway had originally riffed on the idea, without getting it quite right. I think drafts included "It's nice as hell to think so" and "Isn't it nice to think so?" I've been thinking about his final line over the past couple days, thinking about F. Scott Fitzgerald, too, and if there's a relationship between *The Great Gatsby*'s last line ("borne back ceaselessly into the past") and this sentence from the end of *The Sun Also Rises*. Both lines say something central about the human capacity for self-delusion, and how the future never quite serves up solutions to our discontent.

If Hemingway had been like Fitzgerald and added an adverb to tell us how Jake Barnes says that line, what word would he use? How do you think Jake says it?

Is it wistful? Is it cynical? I mean, let's put ourselves in that car with Jake Barnes and Brett Ashley, like we're filmmakers filming the actors saying it. How do you direct them to say it? I think it's a painful, resigned, yet darkly wise admission. This is one of those moments when Hemingway/Barnes step away and they're looking at the human condition, and the particular delusion that true happiness is attainable, and they know more than everybody else.

When I think of the mastery of this novel, it's when Hemingway knew to use his imagination and when to rely on his autobiography. The best example of that is Jake's wound. Can you talk about its function in the novel?

Jake, who is Hemingway's protagonist and the prism through which all the action takes place, is impotent. He's been rendered impotent by a war wound. "Jake" was originally called "Hemingway" in early drafts. Hemingway used the real names of those who inspired his characters in the earliest manuscript, and he was his own inspiration for this main character. But then, all of sudden, somebody with as much masculine bravado as Hemingway renders his character, based on himself, impotent. It was a shocking and unpredictable move. It really made me like Hemingway so much more than I would have otherwise, because it showed that he was willing to compromise his own hyper-masculine image.

Hemingway was also drawing on personal experience. He wasn't impotent, or wounded that way in World War I; however, he was wounded significantly during the war. I think he got something like 230 or 227 bits of shrapnel in him, some very close to *that* area. If one of those pieces of shrapnel had gone the wrong way, he could have been Barnes. So, he's had time since to think about what that would have been like. It's a pretty close brush with a totally different future and a different legacy, a legacy of not being able to have lovers—or children.

—

*"It really made me like Hemingway so much more
than I would have otherwise, because it showed that
he was willing to compromise his own
hyper-masculine image."*

—

In terms of using the wound as a literary device, Hemingway created a removed observer in Jake. By making the character impotent, he is necessarily apart; he can never consummate his relationship with Lady Brett Ashley, the object of his longing. It makes Jake more of an agonized observer. The move was a master-stroke, and personally surprising.

Beyond the war aspect of the wound, doesn't it also parallel Hemingway's own love-triangle, which forms the backdrop to the novel?

In real life, Hemingway had been trotting around Paris with this peculiarly lovely British aristocrat named Lady Duff Twysden who's turned up in town from London. She's already got two lovers in tow when they all go together to Pamplona, Spain, for the bullfights—the trip which eventually inspires *The Sun Also Rises*. Both of those lovers would also inspire characters in the novel, too.

Lady Duff's this very tweedy aristocrat, but there's also something kind of feral about her. Men just adore her, and Hemingway is no exception. Poor Hadley, his wife, is beside herself about this new infatuation. But luckily for Hadley, Lady Duff is always holding Hemingway at arm's length. We don't know for sure, but evidence indicates that Hemingway and Duff's relationship was likely never consummated, and this is not for lack of trying on his part.

Hemingway eventually translated his own relationship with Lady Duff into Jake's relationship with Lady Brett, but in a way that conserves his personal honor. On paper, it's not that Brett is rejecting Jake. Brett wants him desperately, but he just can't consummate their relationship because he's had this terrible thing happen to him and he can't perform. For me, that's a less noble literary use of the war wound, as opposed to using it to create a removed observer.

When I used to look at that famous photo of Hemingway, Hadley, Duff Twysden, and all of them in Pamplona, I always was drawn to the women in particular, and thought about how complicated yet limited their lives were, how little agency they had—especially poor Duff. She epitomizes allure and female fascination in Paris during that time, and while she appears to be controlling half the male expats there, in reality she has no real control over her own life and destiny. In life and in Hemingway's pages, she really didn't have that much agency at all. Her life was just pilfered by him. Some might say her life story was very glamorously rendered and preserved by Hemingway in the novel. But she was devastated by Hemingway's profligate portrayal of her.

Let's jump back to the beginning of *The Sun Also Rises*, and the true-life story behind it. Fitzgerald actually emerges as a crucial character in the making of that novel. Why was he so central?

Fitzgerald saw Hemingway's potential, and he wanted Hemingway to be the best possible version of himself. As a reader of *The Sun Also Rises* and an informal editor on it, along with Hemingway's real editor, Max Perkins, Fitzgerald made crucial edits and suggestions as one of the first readers of the manuscript. He was administering a lot of tough love to Hemingway, saying in essence, "Look, your product has to match your talent. There are so many people who want what you want. Unless you make this the best possible version of your writing, you're not going to get the success you want." He was being tough as hell, but at the same time he was an unwavering champion.

And the backroom wrangling to get Hemingway published, right?

Absolutely. Not only did Fitzgerald wrangle in-house at his own publisher, at Scribner's, to bring Hemingway on board there, but he also paved the way for Hemingway to succeed in other ways. He was one of Hemingway's most vigorous and influential cheerleaders.

And he was also a forerunner for Hemingway, even though their writing styles were very different. It's fair to say that Hemingway defined himself in opposition to Fitzgerald's more floral style, which still had a bit of a Wharton feeling to it. But Fitzgerald was this bright, young writer who had demonstrated with his own work that there was a huge appetite for this kind of cult-of-youth modern literature. He was a pioneer for Hemingway via his own work and celebrity, and then acted as a kingmaker.

Lesley, I wonder what it would have been like for someone to read *The Sun Also Rises* when it first came out in 1926. I start thinking about how artistically and culturally revolutionary Hemingway's language and style really were. Do you think Hemingway's experimentation in this novel can be appreciated in the same way now as it was back in the 1920s?

I don't know how stylistically revolutionary the novel feels for someone picking it up for the first time today. We know that it was a blockbuster when it first came out. I would have loved to have been part of the generation that, a year earlier, had read *The Great Gatsby* and then picked up *The Sun Also Rises* in 1926.

Hemingway's approach with this book was an intentional combination of high-low appeal. It's a gossip-soaked book: sex, booze, naughtiness, adultery. Everybody really does behave very badly in the book. So, it's interesting to people with a more gossipy sensibility, and Hemingway knew that it would have that sort of currency. However, the modern approach to language he employs is highly intellectualized, and he knew that critics would understand what he was up to there and go bananas for it. Then, as now, it's hard to corner both of those markets with the same product. One of my original shortlist titles for my book was *The High-Low.*

As a writer, what was Hemingway's stance toward this "low" material? Did he worry it could cheapen his own art?

He was not ashamed at all of it. In one of his letters, he says, "There's a lot of dope about high society" in the book, and he sees it as a tantalizing selling point for readers who aren't critics. So, he knows he's titillating everybody.

That being said, I don't think you could actually characterize any of the content of the novel itself as "low," because it's all structured and rendered in really specific ways. It all has a purpose. One of the ways Hemingway manages to make the more gossipy, sexual, naughtier parts of the book seem imbued with greater significance is through the biblical title. Once you see everything through that framework, then all of sudden things that seem trashy, or might have seemed more frivolous if, say, Fitzgerald wrote them, have now been imbued with that biblical gravitas. Hemingway's not the first person to do this. Edith Wharton's title *The House of Mirth* is biblical. That's one of the things about Hemingway; he's looking at everybody else's work, he's read everyone, and even if he disapproves of you as a writer and person, he'll still take something from you if he thinks it works.

You call his novel a "masterpiece." You also called it a "blockbuster," which it is. But what makes it a masterpiece?

It *is* a masterpiece, and not just in terms of its style and how it introduced "the Hemingway style." Another way it was masterly was how it made that style commercially accessible and successful for the first time. Other writers had also been up to what Hemingway was up to, in experimenting with stripping down language, or repetition, or stream-of-consciousness. For example, you have Gertrude Stein, an American expat-in-Paris pioneer who is helping to launch all these careers there, but one of her linguistically experimental books only sells something like seventy-seven or seventy-three copies in eighteen months. So, she is not making a go of it.

Hemingway, on the other hand, has done everything right. He's made this successful structure of a book, has finely mastered the pared-down, revolutionary approach to language that he's been laboring over, and now suddenly everyone wants to read it. And it wasn't just about masterful marketing, or its foxy, dark voice-of-a-generation appeal. It also had to do with revolutionizing literature in a way that was electric for readers of all backgrounds and around the world.

One of Hemingway's qualities you really seem to emphasize is his ambition, right?

I'd say Hemingway's ambition is his defining characteristic. I used to contribute regularly to *Vanity Fair*. When it was under (former editor-in-chief) Graydon Carter, it was a hub of outsized ambition. Even though I'd been in close proximity to feverish writerly ambition for much of my professional life, I was still shocked when researching *Everybody Behaves Badly* by the caliber and intensity of Hemingway's ambition, even the extent to which he was so bold and unrepentant about it. He admitted it proudly. Ambition seeped from his letters during *The Sun Also Rises* period. Many of them show him strategizing who could help him leverage his position, who could get him published, who could get him higher visibility. Everything pertained to that. Usually, people try to disguise their ambition a little more, but his was overt. There was absolutely no coyness.

He was also a relentless networker. When he arrived in Paris, he was locked and loaded with letters of introduction to Gertrude Stein and Sylvia Beach, which he had wangled out of writer Sherwood Anderson. Stein and Beach were power brokers in that circle, in that day. This shrewdness was pretty incredible. Hemingway was this quite young guy, too, when he's pursuing all of these connections. I don't feel like I had any idea how to be that savvy about networking when I was his age, but he had it.

>·<

Lesley M. M. Blume is a Los Angeles-based journalist, author, and biographer. Her work has appeared in *Vanity Fair, The New York Times, The Wall Street Journal,* and *The Paris Review,* among many other publications. Her book *Everybody Behaves Badly: The True Story Behind Hemingway's Masterpiece* The Sun Also Rises, was a *New York Times* bestseller. Her book, *Fallout: The Hiroshima Cover-up and the Reporter Who Revealed It to the World,* was a *New York Times* Editor's Choice and Most Notable Book of 2020.

PAULA MCLAIN

What is your one true sentence and why?

My one true sentence is from the last paragraph of *A Moveable Feast:* "There is never any ending to Paris and the memory of each person who has lived in it differs from that of any other."

To end by saying that there is no ending, that's such a provocative move by Hemingway.

It is. It absolutely is. It's crucial to understand that he was working on this memoir at the end of his life. He moved to Paris when he was twenty-two years old in December 1921. The material is all about the beginning of his literary apprenticeship, the way he was building himself as a writer. The pathos of the book comes through the nostalgia and regret as he reimmerses himself in those memories after he has become the most famous living writer in the world. By then he's lost his privacy. He's in old age and has lost much of his memory. He can't sleep anymore. He has nervous trouble. He's had electro-shock therapy. He's had major depressive episodes. He's had two plane crashes. He's battered by life. He's carrying all these memories with him and choosing to revisit Paris as a wellspring of sorts. And I find this last paragraph incredibly optimistic and generous and tender and loving as he returns to Paris as a kind of Eden, with great love and unapologetic idealism.

Hemingway's sentence suggests that just because this is my memory, that doesn't mean it's exactly what happened, or that it's exactly how somebody else would describe it. Where is that line between compelling narrative and strict militant fidelity to what happened?

There can't be a strict militant fidelity to what happened because nobody knows what happened, even if you were in the moment, right? We're always projecting and transposing and disfiguring people. There is no final truth. When I visited the Hemingway holdings at the John F. Kennedy Memorial Library in Boston, I read his handwritten introduction to *A Moveable Feast*, which he wrote obsessively, over and over and over again, crossing things out. I think he struggled with the blurring of those lines. Also, in terms of the subjects in each of those vignettes—other writers, painters, Gertrude Stein, Ford Madox Ford, F. Scott Fitzgerald, his first wife, Hadley Richardson—he's both exposing them and disguising them simultaneously.

So, this is something that you've also faced with your own memoirs as well as when writing historical fiction?

Yes. Because those lines blur all the time.

Do they blur in the same way or is it always different?

They blur in different ways. I think what Hemingway was trying to get at, and certainly what I'm always trying to get at, is the emotional truth of a moment and not the physical truth, or the actual truth, as if someone could determine that. If Paris is an Eden, it's a source of myth. It's the wellspring itself. That's why there is never any end to it. You can return to it again and again.

—

*"What I'm always trying to get at, is the emotional truth
of a moment and not the physical truth, or the actual
truth, as if someone could determine that."*

—

When Hemingway wrote about being up in Michigan, he was able to transplant himself so perfectly that he felt he was experiencing the weather in his mind and in his physical body. He talked about that often in regards to his writing, his ability to go away in his own head and transplant himself back in that place. For the Hemingway who was up in his rooftop garret in Paris, Michigan was also a source or wellspring. There is never any end to those early places either for him.

In your own writing experience, isn't it true that you were never in Paris before you wrote *The Paris Wife*?

That's absolutely right. My impetus for writing *The Paris Wife* was discovering *A Moveable Feast* and becoming completely obsessed with the young Hemingway and his first wife. Because Hemingway didn't expose himself in the book to the degree that he exposed others, I had all these questions about what their lives were like, and I went looking for answers. When I had the initial inspiration, I was dead broke. I had three kids. I had three part-time teaching jobs. I had $600 in my savings account. I could not afford to go to Paris. So, I didn't. I read my way there.

Your novels tend to chronicle strong women. How do you square the women in Hemingway's life, the women that you're drawn to writing, with the obvious misgivings that modern contemporary readers might have with Hemingway?

I sort of carry Hadley in *The Paris Wife* and Martha Gellhorn in *Love and Ruin* in the same crucible side-by-side although they required different levels of empathy. Any time a writer catapults herself into the mind and heart of a character, there is an amalgamation that happens. You become them, they become you, those lines blur. I surrendered myself to writing Hadley's story in her "voice," but I am as unlike Hadley as I could possibly be. I'm much closer to Hemingway or Martha. I like strong women. I really like writing a story where I'm trying to discover how a strong woman becomes herself, what she has to survive to become herself.

You're also dealing with a different Hemingway. He was different with his first wife than with his third wife. Not only are the women different, but Hemingway himself was different with each of them.

Absolutely. It was as if I met Hemingway the way Hadley did, through her eyes at a party in Chicago in 1920. He wasn't the man he would become yet. She saw his insecurity, his self-doubt, his romanticism, his sensitivity. It's not that she was blind to those things. She took those things in stride. So, when somebody hurt his feelings or he would lash out, she understood where his reaction was coming from, because they were kids together. He couldn't put anything over on her. She could see through to the deeper layer.

Does Hemingway's "one true sentence" construct speak to you at all as a writer with your own work, composing just one sentence at a time and looking for the truth in that one sentence?

For me it might differ slightly, but I would say yes. Picture Hemingway in his rooftop garret writing the Nick Adams stories, waiting for that trout to float up from the bottom of the pool. In a way, one true sentence is like that, cutting through all the noise. It's something really that comes from the depths of your subconscious when you're quiet enough, when you still your mind, when you are able to "go away," as he said, to transport yourself to that place where art comes through you. We don't really know what inspiration is.

So yes, I'm always waiting for that and living for that, too. I think if he had one true love and one true devotion, it was to his work and he surrendered entirely to that. I also identify with him there as well. Part of the poignancy of his memoir is the way he was looking back and realizing what he had, and what he'd lost. That we always have to lose Eden. We always have to lose our first loves and our relationship to the purity of the beginning, because we can't unknow what we know. Even the poverty of his early years in Paris, the way he idealized being hungry, burning sticks in his little brazier, all of that. The perfection of that can only be perfect because it's been lost.

≻·≺

PAULA MCLAIN is the author of the *New York Times* bestselling novels, *The Paris Wife, Circling the Sun* and *Love and Ruin.* In 2021, she published *When the Stars Go Dark.*

KIRK CURNUTT

What is your one true sentence and why?

There are so many great examples of well-crafted sentences, but I'm going to go with a sentence that Fitzgerald himself thought was among Hemingway's best. It's the magnificent opening line to "In Another Country" from 1927: "In the fall the war was always there, but we did not go to it any more."

The first thing I would note is for a guy that is sort of known for the thing left out, there's nothing left out in that sentence. It's all a matter of irony and balance. It's two halves of a sentence. There's the war that is omnipresent, but we didn't go to it anymore. It's actually a sentence I've thought about a lot for eighteen years now, because the reality is, we were in a war for nearly twenty years, but at some point we didn't go to it anymore. After Obama's election, Afghanistan simply wasn't newsworthy in the same way that it was in 2001 or 2003. I think it's a great statement about how war really never ends, or there's a moment where war becomes tedious and boring. It's just the new reality. We may have left Afghanistan as of August 2021, but who really believes that war is over?

When they met, had Hemingway read Fitzgerald's earlier fiction and vice versa?

Hemingway actually read Fitzgerald's debut novel *This Side of Paradise* probably when it came out in 1920 and he and Hadley were a little dismissive of it. *This Side of Paradise* has a reputation for being sort of a snotty youth novel, and I think they were probably a little beyond that at that stage of their life. Plus, I think Hemingway was always a little jealous of any writer of his generation who got publicity first. They had been friends through correspondence for a while. I think it was shortly after that he would have read *The Great Gatsby*, but certainly Fitzgerald was already acting as Hemingway's press agent at that time.

If *This Side of Paradise* wasn't along the lines of something that Hemingway was bound to enjoy, is *In Our Time* something that Fitzgerald was likely to enjoy?

Oh, definitely. Hemingway as a reader was probably much more bound to his own values. He tended to enjoy the things that were like his own traits. He was not fond of excessive rhetoric or scrollwork ornamentation in other writers just as he wasn't fond of it in his own. But Fitzgerald was a little broader, and I think he understood the way that writers were unique talents, that they were individual, and that they all had their own voices. He certainly understood the greatness of those Hemingway stories.

A lot of what we think of when we think of Hemingway and Fitzgerald is due to Hemingway getting the last word. Fitzgerald made the enormous mistake of dying before Hemingway, which allowed Hemingway to write about him in his memoirs. What is the role of *A Moveable Feast* in our enduring notion of their friendship?

I've always thought of those chapters on Fitzgerald in *A Moveable Feast* as about the sweetest gutting you could ever give somebody. It's really a master class in sentimental evisceration.

How so?

Well, on the one hand there is genuine affection that comes through. I don't think that Hemingway ever lost his—it doesn't quite rise to admiration—but I would say his awareness, that Fitzgerald was an innate talent. We have a tendency to think of Fitzgerald as the Icarus of American literature; he flew too close to the sun. That's certainly the imagery that Hemingway plays with. Again, it ties into the notion that Fitzgerald was all of forty-four when he died of a heart attack, but in many people's minds, he might as well have been eighty. He was that out of fashion. His world seemed that remote from 1940 by the time that Hemingway started writing those sketches, probably in 1956 or 1957, somewhere in there. Hemingway had been through basically a decade of watching "the Fitzgerald revival" take steam. He was constantly besieged for requests for interviews about Fitzgerald.

—

"It's all a matter of irony and balance."

—

The bad thing about being the first to die is that you're the first to die. But the good thing about that is you become the subject or sort of the center point of everybody else's memories. I think Hemingway grew to resent very much that people were starting to revive Fitzgerald. I think he really saw *A Moveable Feast*, not as settling a score, but kind of punching a few holes in the hype that was associated with the Fitzgerald legend by that period.

Hemingway starts his "Scott Fitzgerald" chapter in *A Moveable Feast* with that famous epigraph: "His talent was as natural as the pattern that was made by the dust on a butterfly's wings." Rather than mention Fitzgerald's writing or career, here Hemingway focuses on his "talent," a word that people might not necessarily associate with Hemingway.

Yeah. It's kind of a difference between talent and craft. Always the traditional knock on Fitzgerald was he was an intuitive writer, but undisciplined. He had a sort of natural grace. He could write these long, moving kinds of passages. It was all spontaneous, and it came out of his interest in the Romantics, his identification with writers like Keats. If you go and read early Fitzgerald, early Fitzgerald is the Fitzgerald that became famous. There's really no difference between his college writing and *This Side of Paradise*. In fact, that pretty much was his college writing. Some of those early stories that he collects in his first two collections of stories were stuff that he published while at Princeton.

Hemingway's the exact opposite. If you look at it, by any measure, Hemingway's juvenilia is awful. To think that the same man who would write "Soldier's Home" or any of the Nick Adams stories was writing so badly just a few years before is amazing.

It's easy in any discussion of Hemingway and Fitzgerald to see a clear dichotomy of Hemingway having one set of interests and one writing style and Fitzgerald having the opposite. But if we picture this as a Venn diagram, where is the overlap?

It starts with the fact that they're both Midwesterners. Then, I think they're both also haunted by a sense of loss. Fitzgerald didn't scratch the surface enough when he claimed that Hemingway wrote with the authority of success, because how much of Hemingway is really about loss? They're both sort of defined by the initial loss of a love. Ginevra King jilted Fitzgerald for not being wealthy enough, and Agnes von Kurowsky jilted Hemingway. Those are both the broken hearts and wounded egos that launched their careers. I also think when we talk about addictions, they shared that. We do need to look more at the commonalities of their experiences than the things that set them apart.

➤·◄

Kirk Curnutt is the Executive Director of the F. Scott Fitzgerald Society and serves on the board of the Ernest Hemingway Foundation Society. He is also professor of English at Troy University in Montgomery, Alabama. He is the author of fourteen books of fiction and criticism, most recently *The New Hemingway Studies* (co-edited with Suzanne del Gizzo). He has also helped develop two literary podcasts: *Master the 40* (a show focused on Fitzgerald and co-hosted by Robert Trogdon) and *Great American Novel* (with Scott Yarbrough).

CRAIG JOHNSON

ONE TRUE SENTENCE FROM
"The Snows of Kilimanjaro"

What is your one true sentence and why?

You can't ask a writer to do something without them rewriting the rules! I did find myself doing a little bit of a rewrite on that question. Let's say it's a couple of sentences, but it illustrates one of the things I find truly amazing about Hemingway's work and kind of deals with that honesty that he discusses. It's the epigraph from the beginning of "The Snows of Kilimanjaro": "Kilimanjaro is a snow-covered mountain 19,710 feet high, and is said to be the highest mountain in Africa. Its western summit is called the Masai 'Ngàje Ngài,' the House of God. Close to the western summit there is the dried and frozen carcass of a leopard. No one has explained what the leopard was seeking at that altitude."

What does that epigraph say to you?

Well, it's almost more what it doesn't say. The thing I really enjoy about it is the ambiguity. It's a statement; it's a strong statement. It gives you a ton of information before you even start the short story, but it also leaves something to the imagination, and I think that that's one of the things about Hemingway's writing that a lot of people tend to overlook. They always talk about the precision of his writing. They always talk about the direct quality of his writing. He also did an awful lot of things where he would take a fact or he would take an emotion or a piece of dialogue and just toss it out there and let you make of it what you will. That sounds relatively simple. It sounds like, "Oh, I'm sure every writer does that." No, they don't. A lot of them don't have that kind of courage. That's the term that I would use. He was an absolutely courageous writer in the sense that, in searching for the truth, he was willing to go out on that thin ice.

What's the difference between a courageous writer and one without courage?

I think that Hemingway addresses that. It's that truth and honesty that you're shooting for. Then take that even a step further. You could look at it as a universality of the human condition in many ways, trying to find something within this story in order to find something within the words that's going to resonate with not just a select group but with anybody that reads it. To have that ambiguity within the writing is a daring thing. It's very simple to sit down and write the facts and nothing but the facts, but to leave something to the reader's imagination, you're enjoining them to step out onto that thin ice along with you and trust you in the telling of this story.

And Hemingway was a master at that. It's a marvelous way to start out that short story. You can talk about the symbolism of it. You can talk about how the snow means death or the leopard is the human condition or the spirit of humanity and all these different things. Yeah, it could be. It could also be a dead leopard up at about 19,000 feet. So, it opens it up for a lot of opportunities that do require a certain amount of literary courage.

—

*"He was an absolutely courageous writer in
the sense that, in searching for the truth, he
was willing to go out on that thin ice."*

—

In my own personal experience along those lines, I'm a big one for outlining my work to death. I tend to refer to what I write as socially responsible crime fiction in the sense that I'm trying to say something, there's a message I'm trying to get across with each book. I'm not just looking to pile up bodies like cordwood. I've got something to say, and the difficulty is that if you start out as a big outliner sometimes you can easily get hidebound by those outlines.

Sometimes you get to the point where, boy, you're not going to get away from those outlines at all. What you discover is that the more you develop as a writer, the more you develop in your abilities, the more you start to trust those improvisational moments that might present themselves. What you discover is, in those improvisational moments, something sparks, something happens, something different, something you hadn't accounted for to take you somewhere where the writing really becomes something marvelous.

Is courage something that the writer is born with? Is it something that the writer gains and, therefore, could lose? If you look at your shelf full of books, do you believe that you were more honest in one than in the other?

The answer to your question is: all three. Of course, there are some who are born with it, some who intuitively accomplish or acquire it. Then, yeah, if you're not careful, it's like a sharp blade. You can cut yourself with it, or it can get dull. You have to make sure your tools stay sharp, or else you can become repetitious, predictable, formulaic, all of those things.

I think it's even more of a danger whenever you write a series of books. You need to reinvent the wheel with every single book. You need to try and do something different with every single book. If you're not doing that, then you're going to end up with a drawer full of dull knives. Then, after a certain period of time, you even forget how to sharpen them, and you don't know how to use those tools. So, that's part of that courage that we discussed: you can't let your guard down. You have to try and do something different every time, or else why bother writing it?

If you were going from an outline, is that more of a conceptual, structural, plot-driven organizing principle as opposed to seizing on one true sentence?

You use it as a map, but there are going to be opportunities to disregard that map. You keep it in the glove box just in case you get lost and can't remember, "What was the meaning of this book? Why was I writing this?" I do think that the day-to-day part, the part where you sit down and look into that vast expanse of whiteness, that Arctic tundra that stretches out before you, which can be just as intimidating as a glacier or a snowcap peak, you have to attack those on a moment-to-moment basis. You can make all the preparations in the world and then get ready, because things are going to change along the way, and that's good because it challenges you. It makes you have to rise to the occasion on a day-to-day basis, on an hour-to-hour basis, on a moment-to-moment basis, on a sentence basis, on a word basis.

To go back to the last sentence of the epigraph, "No one has explained what the leopard was seeking at that altitude." What do you think it was seeking?

We're all looking for something. We're all trying to find something. And sometimes that can take you to some far-flung regions, not only frontiers, geographically, but emotional and intellectual frontiers.

➤•◄

CRAIG JOHNSON is the *New York Times* bestselling author of the *Longmire* mysteries, the basis for the hit Netflix original series *Longmire*. He is the recipient of the Western Writers of America Spur Award for fiction, the Mountains and Plains Booksellers Award for fiction, the Nouvel Observateur Prix du Roman Noir, and the Prix SNCF du Polar. His novella *Spirit of Steamboat* was the first One Book Wyoming selection. He lives in Ucross, Wyoming, population twenty-five.

MARC K. DUDLEY

A Farewell to Arms and Green Hills of Africa

What is your one true sentence and why?

Let me start with the easy one. This is a few sentences into the first chapter of
A Farewell to Arms: "The trunks of the trees too were dusty and the leaves fell
early that year and we saw the troops marching along the road and the dust
rising and leaves, stirred by the breeze, falling and the soldiers marching and
afterward the road bare and white except for the leaves."

And my second sentence, from *Green Hills of Africa,* is about halfway
through the narrative. In it, Hemingway's reflecting on the hunt and he's
also reflecting on just life in general, art, and the Gulf Stream in America.
The sentence begins with: "That something I cannot yet define completely
but the feeling comes when you write well and truly of something and know
impersonally you have written in that way and those who are paid to read it
and report on it do not like the subject so they say it is all a fake, yet you know
its value absolutely ... that stream will flow, as it has flowed, after the Indians, after the Spaniards, after the British, after the Americans and after all
the Cubans and all the systems of governments, the richness, the poverty, the
martyrdom, the sacrifice and the venality and the cruelty are all gone as the
high-piled scow of garbage, bright-colored, white-flecked, ill-smelling, now

tilted on its side, spills off its load into the blue water, turning it a pale green to a depth of four or five fathoms as the load spreads across the surface, the sinkable part going down and the flotsam of palm fronds, corks, bottles, and used electric light globes, seasoned with an occasional condom or a deep floating corset, the torn leaves of a student's exercise book, a well-inflated dog, the occasional rat, the no-longer-distinguished cat..." And it goes on and on and on for another seven or eight lines.

That's a terrific one. I think of the back of the Scribner's paperbacks, where it says that Hemingway was "known for his tough, terse prose." Both of those are magnificent sentences, but they're not what you would think of as typically Hemingwayesque. Is that fair to say?

It's fair to say, and I think you've articulated my reasoning well. My rationale lies in your question. I would say that the first sentence is just sort of a brief example of what you get in the second sentence, or a briefer one; however, neither one comports with what we expect of Hemingway. Even that first example is not necessarily the "tough, terse prose" you mention, or the classic short declarative sentences we come to expect of him. It's funny you suggest the Scribner's description, because I usually start with the publisher's declaration, too. As I initiate my class into all things Hemingway, they have expectations, and these things fly in the face of those expectations. I think they're fantastic examples of all the things that Hemingway can do and just how complex an artist he really was.

As we talk about the ways in which Hemingway defies our expectation, he is the poster child for the dead white male. To view him in racial terms or his work in racial terms is particularly fascinating. I'm thinking of *Playing in the Dark: Whiteness and the Literary Imagination*, where Toni Morrison powerfully examines Hemingway's treatment of race.

Toni Morrison had the unique position of being not just a practiced reader along with us, but a practiced critic and a practiced writer. Part and parcel of her exploration in *Playing in the Dark* is Morrison's climbing into the skin of a writer and reimagining all of those American idealistic spaces from the vantage point of a writer. Why does the writer do what he or she does? That provides a unique perspective and angle on Hemingway, about whom she's very mixed. As was I when I first started reading him.

I came to Hemingway looking at him as this grand conundrum. I saw *Green Hills of Africa* as something vastly more than a spectacular adventure or an interesting recount of that adventure. I remember just asking myself, "Why am I so bothered by this work, aside from the obvious?" I was perplexed but also transfixed by lots of things. I was mainly interested in his use of language in relation to his construction of race and his complex construction of identity politics. That was interesting to me.

I noticed there was a pattern. He was talking about these otherwise unmentioned voices, entities, quantities; he's talking about these people during his hunts in East Africa and saying something greater about race. So, if I had one bone to pick with Morrison—maybe somewhere halfway through her indictment of him, when she says that Hemingway has no need for the African American presence beyond his own imagination—it would be her wholesale dismissal of just what it is that Hemingway does with race. I just remember thinking, that isn't necessarily true.

Is Morrison saying that it's a blind spot and you're arguing that Hemingway is doing it intentionally?

In a nutshell, yeah. I'd say that would be it, because Morrison also uses phraseology like "slips of the pen," or something like that. I think that everything that Hemingway did was deliberate, and that is not to discount the racist implications of his texts, certainly. But I think that there was a lot of deliberation going on. Hemingway's racialized textual moments are more than just afterthoughts.

As I reconsider all of Hemingway's treatment of race, I think of gratuitous examples in *The Sun Also Rises*. Can we make a pro-Hemingway argument for why it would make the novel better to have a description of the drummer with some fairly shocking racial coding? Is it not gratuitous?

As a scholar of color, I can't necessarily come out on the side of advocating for this and making it necessarily a better work in this instance. But I think your question is a valid question. Are the descriptions necessary?

—

"I was mainly interested in his use of language in relation to his construction of race and his complex construction of identity politics."

—

Morrison talks about things like the implication of the drummer in *Playing in the Dark* where she lays out what she calls a formula for what American writers do when they engage with race. They do things like fetishize race, use repeated images, or set up spatial markers to separate races, separate white from black, for example. Hemingway is not exceptional here. Morrison also says that there's often a very healthy helping of metonymy going on. That's exactly what you get in the case of the drummer in *The Sun Also Rises*, who is described as being sort of "all teeth and lips"—that racial coding to which you alluded. You see the same thing in the short story "The Battler" where Hemingway engages with what I would effectively call racial coding, where he reads the African American characters, through the eyes of Nick Adams, as being necessarily African American based on the way he walks and the way he talks.

The question I ask in my own study, at the end, is for future scholars: "What do we know about Brett's relationship with this African American drummer?" Obviously, they know each other intimately, just based on the language she uses to describe him. She says he's "a great friend of mine" and he seems to look at her as though they have an intimate relationship. So, maybe there are valid questions to ask just in the very brief encounter that we see there, based on race and the racial coding that goes on.

That's maybe giving Hemingway way too much credit, but we're talking about an artist who's well-studied, well-versed, well-read. I'm also guessing that some of his audience would meet him halfway and know the story behind Tiger Flowers, for example, whose engagement with modern society at that point would be considered to be unjust or unfair. You see that as a thematic constant in several of Hemingway's works. If we think about those kinds of instances as being references to a greater story Hemingway's telling about race relations and American politics, if the reader is able to meet Hemingway and the work halfway or do a little bit of the work themselves, the mining of those stories can be fruitful endeavors. Hemingway (and I'm going to give him a little bit of credit here), I think he's betting on that.

➤·◄

MARC K. DUDLEY is a professor at North Carolina State University. He is the author of *Understanding James Baldwin* and *Hemingway, Race, and Art: Bloodlines and the Color Line.*

CARL P. EBY

ONE TRUE SENTENCE FROM

the "Paris 1922" sketches

What is your one true sentence and why?

I went back to something that Hemingway never published, but that Carlos Baker published in 1969, a little series of six individual sentences that Hemingway wrote and titled "Paris 1922." Baker's assertion was that this is when Hemingway began working on the concept of one true sentence.

Each one takes the form of: *I saw x*. I would argue that this is when Hemingway became Hemingway. These are 1922 sentences. He had published, at this point, "A Divine Gesture" (which doesn't even sound remotely like "Hemingway" as we know him) and he had also written "Up in Michigan," but that's all he had written before "Paris 1922."

Here's the sentence: "I have seen the one legged street walker who works the Boulevard Madeleine between the Rue Cambon and Bernheim Jeune's limping along the pavement through the crowd on a rainy night with a beefy red-faced Episcopal clergyman holding an umbrella over her."

There's an apocryphal story about Hemingway writing, "For Sale: baby shoes, never worn," right? The single-sentence story. But I think this sentence from "Paris 1922" is a much better story. It implies where he's going to go with the vignettes of *In Our Time*. I think it's a one-sentence vignette. What I like is the compression of it, the vivid imagery, the kind of objective correlatives that he'll talk about in *Death in the Afternoon*, those things that make a sentence produce an emotion, and the psychological charge of it. I also love Hemingway's attention to the details and symbolic meaning of material reality.

Like the Rue Cambon. Why the Rue Cambon? That's right in back of the Ritz Hotel. That's where Coco Chanel had her couture house. You read this sentence, about this one-legged streetwalker, and you're thinking about a really seedy district. But no, this is a ritzy district.

Bernheim-Jeune is an art museum?

Right, a gallery that was selling all the avant-garde artists. They represented Paul Cézanne, Henri Matisse, Amedeo Modigliani, Marie Laurencin, Fernand Léger—all of them were represented by Bernheim-Jeune. So, here is a tension. This whole sentence is structured by a series of tensions and ambiguities that are gorgeous.

Madeleine, of course, is the French word for Magdalene. So, we have the prostitute on the Rue Madeleine, and right next to Bernheim-Jeune is the Church of the Magdalene, which actually looks like a Greek temple.

You've got, on the one hand, an Episcopal clergyman with his umbrella over the prostitute, and you could do a very sentimental reading of that if you want: here's the clergyman looking out for this poor prostitute. Whereas, with his red face, I think it's implied that that's *not* what's going on here. It's so suggestive in a really creepy and disturbing way.

—

"What I like is the compression … the vivid imagery, the kind of objective correlatives … those things that make a sentence produce an emotion."

—

And then when you think about the Magdalene, I mean, she's a true servant of Christ in spite of being a prostitute, and here you've got the Episcopal clergyman, supposedly the true servant of Christ, but he is probably picking up the prostitute. And he's an *Episcopal* clergyman—an American, in other words—not someone an American reader can dismiss as alien or other. You could read this sentence in any combination of ways.

The story turns on these tensions. There are levels and layers that structure the narrative of just this single sentence.

One of the qualities that Hemingway is always associated with is objectivity. Is he tipping his hand here and saying, "I'm going to satirize religion or a streetwalker or Paris," or is he playing it right down the middle as an ideal journalist would?

I doubt he actually saw exactly this. It's too perfect in all of the details. I don't think it's historical in that sense. I think it is as objectively presented as he could present it, but it's got all of these ambiguities buried within it that he's going to make us think about. Bernheim-Jeune is selling this avant-garde art for money, right next to the temple. So, is that prostitution, too? But he doesn't tip his hand and tell you, "Oh, you've got to read it this way, or you read it that way."

What does "true" mean in the context of one true sentence?

I think he's talking specifically about the simple declarative sentence and also a way of beginning a story, without the feeling of introducing or presenting something. If you think about the beginning of "On the Quai at Smyrna," you get a sentence like, "The strange thing was, he said, how they screamed every night at midnight." Boom, you are in this story. I mean, it's a great first sentence. There's not the feeling of, well, "When I was a child ..." you know, that kind of lame introductory strategy. This immediacy is really important, particularly to his early aesthetic when he's very interested in the compression of meaning.

>-·-←

CARL P. EBY is President of the Ernest Hemingway Foundation and Society and author of *Hemingway's Fetishism: Psychoanalysis and the Mirror of Manhood*. He is the co-editor of *Hemingway's Spain: Imagining the Spanish World*. A Professor of English at Appalachian State University, he is currently working on a volume devoted to *The Garden of Eden* for Kent State University Press's Reading Hemingway series.

ERIK NAKJAVANI

ONE TRUE SENTENCE FROM
Green Hills of Africa

What is your one true sentence and why?

The sentence appears in the first chapter of *Green Hills of Africa*: "There is a fourth and fifth dimension that can be gotten." In prose, that is. Hemingway accidentally meets a former plantation owner, an Austrian by the name of Kandinsky, and they have a conversation, which leads them to a discussion of literature in general and narrative prose in particular. Hemingway tells him only that he believes there is a fourth and fifth dimension that a narrative prose writer might attain. He takes it for granted that Kandinsky already knows about the three-dimensional Euclidean spatial dimensions—width, height, and depth. So, he doesn't get into descriptions of these dimensions.

Hemingway published *Green Hills of Africa* in 1935. By this time, someone like him would surely have been aware of Einstein's four-dimensional spatio-temporal theory of reality. Hence, he only mentions the fourth dimension of time and then goes beyond it to the fifth dimension. It's interesting that he finds having luck—"if any one is serious enough and has luck"—a necessity to succeed at creating the fifth dimension of narrative prose. In the context of Abrahamic religions (Judaism, Christianity, and Islam), the luck needed to

72

achieve the fifth dimension would be the religious condition of being in the state of grace. I used to say to my students that there was also a kind of Freudian interpretation of having luck or being lucky. That simply means that one is engaged in what aligns itself with fulfilling instinctive, unconscious desires, where all creative forces originate.

Is Hemingway talking about these extra dimensions on a sentence-by-sentence level, or is he talking about it conceptually, like, "I'm going to write a book that has fourth and fifth dimensions"?

He places it at the center of the immediate concrete reality of our lived experiences of our lifeworld and its potential for creative transformations. As phenomenology teaches us, that is the primary basis of all human perception of subjective-objective reality. Through it, Hemingway goes beyond the known; looking to capture the as-yet-unknown through the experientially-known. He does so by expanding the possibilities and potentials of the experiential. He would like to see it intimate something of what is at present beyond our ability to comprehend. These considerations imaginatively create a certain kind of narrative prose, reality of their own, which I think of as the fifth dimension of narrative prose, as virtual reality.

—

"Hemingway said that you could actually go beyond the 'true' as we ordinarily perceive it."

—

Now one might legitimately ask, "How can all this be accomplished? How do we do it?" Structural linguistics can help us here. It takes us to the lexical plane of the words we're using and the considerable freedom of choice they offer. Then on the syntactic plane, there is considerable grammatical flexibility or malleability. Finally, on the semantic level we reach the unlimited pluralities of meaning and their immense interpretive possibilities or hermeneutics. They are all subject to all kinds of creative and imaginative alterations.

Your most recent work was on fictionalized autobiography in *Under Kilimanjaro*. Your one true sentence is from *Green Hills of Africa*, which also plays with the notion of fiction versus nonfiction. So, where does truth or fiction come into play in this discussion of dimensions?

Excellent question, truly. It takes us to the very heart of the mystery of both. One can say there is always contingent objective truth, which one can perceive, extract, and develop. This makes manifest the freedom, the flexibility that language gives us. Hemingway said that you could actually go beyond the "true" as we ordinarily perceive it. It sounds somewhat exaggerated. I believe by that he meant where one can create something novel that surpasses lived experiences but is totally rooted in it, it acquires the potential of being truer than true. This is really a very extraordinary thing to me, this notion of freedom. It allows imagination to envelop us and to create something magical that could only be taking place in the spatiotemporal dimensions of the imaginable. Perhaps I'm exaggerating, but I really feel that way, that there is a notion of freedom within the predetermined that the imagination can make malleable, and that gives one a certain kind of exaltation. Hemingway lifts you up to this level. I call it virtual reality for this very reason.

That response makes me think of a letter that Hemingway wrote to his father in 1925, ten years before *Green Hills of Africa*. In a March 20, 1925 letter, Hemingway tells his father, "You see I'm trying in all my stories to get the feeling of the actual life across—not to just depict life—or criticize it—but to actually make it alive. So that when you have read something by me you actually experience the thing .... It is only by showing both sides—

three dimensions and if possible four that you can write the way I want to." This has to be one of his earliest aesthetic pronouncements, and he's already talking about this concept.

Precisely. And to me it is almost a sense of ecstasy to realize this!

Do you view this artistic approach as Hemingway's career-long project, or did it evolve or even fall away?

I do think that what I consider as his concept of virtual reality of prose narrative came early in his career and stayed with him throughout his writing life. In our discussion of virtual reality as embodiment of lived experiences in the imaginal sphere, autobiography plays a decisive, formative, and informative role in Hemingway's works of fictional narratives. Consequently, I find your reference to Hemingway's 1925 letter to his father to be most salutary. Or should I more appropriately say "lucky." Nearly a century ago, he elucidated the development of a virtual reality as an innovative style of prose narrative, entirely his own, which has been recognized as such worldwide.

I would say it acquired a complex, significant, and signifying ontology and epistemology of its own. Today we clearly recognize it in works of arts, literature as well as in contemporary sciences. Accordingly, I would say most of Hemingway's fiction, even some of his journalism, at their best, partake of a modality of virtual reality. His genius comes forth in this fifth dimension of prose, for which there is no algorithm.

ERIK NAKJAVANI is Professor Emeritus of Humanities at the University of Pittsburgh. He was a founding member of the Hemingway Society. His latest publication on Hemingway is "Theory and Practice of Fictionalized Autobiography: Hemingway's *Under Kilimanjaro*" published in *The Norman Mailer Review*.

STACY KEACH

The Sun Also Rises

What is your one true sentence and why?

I can read you a paragraph from *The Sun Also Rises*: "When he had finished his work with the muleta and was ready to kill, the crowd made him go on. They did not want the bull killed yet, they did not want it to be over. Romero went on. It was like a course in bull-fighting. All the passes he linked up, all completed, all slow, templed and smooth. There were no tricks and no mystifications. There was no brusqueness. And each pass as it reached the summit gave you a sudden ache inside. The crowd did not want it ever to be finished."

It's so evocative. I love that "all completed, all slow." What a way to describe a bullfight. It's just extraordinary. He found the poetry, not only in his soul, but in life.

What role did Hemingway play in your reading as a young man?

I was not a very good English student in either high school or at the beginning of my college career. One of the first experiences I had that awakened me to a new realm of literature was Hemingway's *In Our Time*. I read that as a freshman, and it seemed to me like he was talking to my soul. I felt like my thought processes and his were in sync. It was a really extraordinary experience.

What was it about reading *In Our Time* that felt extraordinary?

It was the style of writing. I felt like he was emulating my thought process stylistically. Some of Hemingway's subjects for me were more interesting than others, but it was the style that really captured my imagination.

As someone who has read all of Hemingway's short stories for an audiobook, did you find that his style left a lot open to interpretation? The dialogue isn't really coaxed. He's not telling you exactly how someone said something.

Exactly. He doesn't use a lot of adjectives in that respect. He's not biased in one way or another. His prose is descriptive in the most evocative way. I'm thinking specifically of passages from *Death in the Afternoon* that I read as Hemingway in the one-man play, *Pamplona*. His description of the bullfights, for example, is just extraordinary. He's struggling in the play to write one true sentence. He's trying to finish a sentence. He's trying to write a piece about Antonio Ordoñez, and he's stuck. He's got writer's block. In order to break this block and to awaken his senses once again, he has to revisit the demons of his past, his wives, his mother, his relatives, his relationships, and finally he does come up with it.

Can we draw some associations between writing and acting? In your autobiography, you express an antipathy towards actors who understate a moment.

Yeah, I think that may have come from one of my classes I was teaching. It's just to tell young actors not to be afraid to overdo it. Don't be afraid to go there. You can always tone it down, but to get to it is the important thing so that you can express the fullness of whatever you're trying to do.

Is there a risk in a writer or an actor being so consistently understated? If the writer or actor gets it just right, even though it's understated, could it work even better than an excess of emotion?

Yes. I think if you hit it, if you get it right, then it's great. But, for an actor specifically, I think it's always good to explore the extremes of an emotional moment. "I love you," for example. I mean, there are a million ways to say that. I love to see actors explore all the various ways of doing that, and then to have it at your disposal. You can call on either one. In some respects, the same holds true for a writer. Hemingway was always very proud that he used his imagination. He made things up.

Is there a danger for actors in overthinking a moment?

Overthinking is always a problem. Whether it's acting or playing golf, over-thinking is never good during a performance. Overthinking is not bad when you're preparing, but when you're in the process of performing, you're flying; you're just doing it. It's all there because you've already prepared for it. It's all there.

What was your approach to recording Hemingway's short stories? Every time you read a line of dialogue is an act of interpretation. Did you find that to be daunting or exciting?

A lot of times I will not look at something. I will not read something before I'm going to record it because I want the short story to be a surprise to me, and I want that to be reflected in my voice when I'm reading it for the first time. That engages the listener the same way I am engaged as the narrator. Other times when it's more complicated, or something that is very well known, a short story like "The Snows of Kilimanjaro," I would reread that many times before I would actually record it to find a way of how to interpret that ending.

—

"He found the poetry, not only in his soul,
but in life."

—

When we were shooting the mini-series and we were in Africa, I could see Kilimanjaro and it really grabbed me. I reread that story with different eyes. The thing that impressed me about it was it was majestic, amazing, regal. I thought that there were elements of that in his story, in the way he treated his characters.

You're somebody who plays great men, in the sense of having outsized heroic or anti-heroic personalities. Does Hemingway qualify along those lines? And how do you prepare for that kind of scope?

He does. He definitely is in that category, and one of the reasons why I was drawn to doing him as a one-man presentation was because it really absorbs all of my energies in terms of vulnerability and also just outlandish showmanship. I don't consciously prepare for that. For me, research is one of the most enjoyable facets of my work because I get to learn about the person, his relationships, the history of the period, the era, the time which the person comes from. That to me is exciting. I love that. It's stimulating, and that's the trigger for my imaginative juices to start flowing and to determine how I'm going to interpret a character or a role or a moment.

How did you justify Hemingway's temper?

I didn't. It wasn't necessarily a justification as it was the expression of his temper. I mean, we all have tempers to varying degrees, and that kind of lack of control that he experienced, I think, was largely due to his drinking. I think there was a definite connection with his drinking and that side of his personality that was not so pleasant, particularly with women. It has to do also with his relationship with his parents. His relationship with his mother, particularly, was so poisonous. One of my favorite sentences of Hemingway was when he stood there describing his father and his mother and the fact that they had so little in common. He said his dad had about as much in common with her as a coyote has with a white French poodle.

Did you find him to be a man that you understood or a man that you condemned? Did you detest certain aspects of Hemingway or love other aspects?

It's very dangerous for an actor to make value judgements, at least if they're negative value judgments, to start judging a character's actions particularly when you're playing bad guys. A lot of times, actors try to justify the badness that they're playing by thinking either there's some flaw in their character, or there's some vulnerability, something that doesn't paint them in black, Iago-like terms, but that's a big mistake. If a character is Iago, that's how you have to play him.

➤·◄

In the ninety or so years since Hemingway's work has been interpreted for different artistic media, two actors have made the greatest contribution: Gary Cooper and STACY KEACH. For

Hemingway fans, Keach is recognizable as the man who played Hemingway in the 1988 miniseries, *Hemingway.* He also undertook the prodigious task of narrating the complete short stories of Hemingway for Simon & Schuster in 2002. Most recently, Keach starred in the well-received one-act play about Hemingway, *Pamplona.*

VERNA KALE

"Soldier's Home"

What is your one true sentence and why?

This is a sentence from Hemingway's short story "Soldier's Home." It comes toward the end of the story, when Harold Krebs is with his mother. She asks him, "Don't you love your mother?" and he says, "No." She says to him, and this is my one true sentence: "I'm your mother... I held you next to my heart when you were a tiny baby." I wouldn't say from an aesthetic viewpoint that this is my favorite sentence, or that it's the most beautiful sentence Hemingway ever wrote. It is one that has always stuck out for me, even bothered me. It's very moving. At the same time, it makes me very uncomfortable.

Tell me about your reaction to that moment in the story. What about it makes you feel uncomfortable?

This is a sentence that makes me feel things, and it makes me not want to feel things. It almost makes you ashamed to feel things. As a reader, it's kind of a painful sentence. As a mother, I think this sentence is very painful. You know, we have Harold Krebs, who has just returned from World War I, who is struggling with the aftereffects of war, the return to civilian life, and, in this conversation, the relationship with his own mother. She's struggling too, and there's a lot of tension there between these two people. The question in the sentence is about love and about that relationship.

Is Mrs. Krebs giving Harold a guilt trip intentionally? Or is this as authentic a plea as a mother could possibly give to an emotionally distant son?

I think that the character of Harold Krebs's mother has been misunderstood. She's seen as sanctimonious and emotionally manipulative. I don't feel like that's what's actually going on here in this story. She loves him very much. This is her child. He, at one time, was a tiny baby, and she really did hold him next to her heart. She feels that love for him. It's important to accept that at face value. She's not trying to make him feel bad. Why would she do that? This is legitimately a plea from her. She wants her son back.

It's important to get away from the idea that Harold Krebs and Hemingway have any kind of biographical similarities. Harold Krebs is not Ernest Hemingway. Mrs. Krebs is not Ernest's mother, Grace Hemingway. By default, people have read this story as autobiographical, but Hemingway and Harold Krebs don't really have much in common. In our haste, we overlook just how different they are, and we can really misunderstand the damage that's been done to Harold. Harold is a college boy. He had gone to a Methodist college. He was in a fraternity. Neither of those details applies to Hemingway. What they do tell us about Krebs, on the other hand, is that when he left for the war, he was following a pretty conservative, somewhat unremarkable, straight-and-narrow path. He went to college; he was a Protestant; he was a frat boy. For whatever reason, he enlisted and went away with the Marines. When he comes back two years later, he's changed.

Before you go into how the war was a crucible experience for Krebs, didn't it also change Hemingway? Why shouldn't we read their war experiences in a similar way?

Well, let's consider some of the differences between Hemingway and Krebs. Hemingway was definitely traumatized by his war wound. You shouldn't underplay the importance of his wounding along the Piave River. Philip Young made that such an important cornerstone of Hemingway's scholarship early on. At the same time, Hemingway saw some other really dreadful things. One of his first tasks in the war was to clean up the body parts that got blown against a fence when a munitions factory exploded.

His letters from this time, though, are so odd because they are very energetic and almost jovial. You might argue that he's writing home and trying to make sure his parents are not worried, but these letters have that authentic Hemingway spirit in them. It was no doubt terrible, but also kind of a great adventure for him. He spent a good part of the war in the hospital recovering and had an amazing friendship-turned-love-affair with the nurse Agnes von Kurowsky.

Harold had a much different experience. Krebs is in France and Germany. Hemingway's in Italy. Actually, at the time Krebs is in Europe, Hemingway is in high school. But later, Hemingway's in Italy. Krebs thinks back on this photo of himself standing beside the Rhine River with some girls, and there's that other great passage: "The German girls are not beautiful. The Rhine does not show in the picture." So, he's in combat and occasionally sleeping with women who don't even speak his language, who are probably sex workers. Meanwhile, Hemingway's recovering in hospital and has this massive love affair that was possibly slightly one-sided, it turns out, but to him was just this amazing experience. Also, by 1924, when the story was written, Hemingway still had a pretty good relationship with his parents. There's just not a lot that lines up biographically there. The story is a real outlier among the stories in *In Our Time* because it is so different from Hemingway's own experience.

How does Mrs. Krebs respond to the way Harold has come home changed?

Mrs. Krebs, she doesn't really understand that change. She tries to understand, but she doesn't know what her son went through. How could she? Harold won't talk about it. She asks about it, but she doesn't understand enough to really listen, and her attention kind of wanders. The people who do talk about the war have gone back to their normal lives, and she wants the same for her son. I don't think that's necessarily a bad thing. She wants him to get back to the way things were before: the boy who was smart enough to go to college, the boy who's popular enough to pledge a fraternity, the boy who can get a job. Why shouldn't she want those things? Now, she does have some sympathy for him. She's not asking him to go back to college. She's not asking him to get a "good" job. She actually says, "All work is honorable." She just wants him to do something, an honest day's work. She's trying to give him the kind of things that he would have liked before the war, like letting him take the family's car out. I think people see that as showing how little her concerns are compared to what he's been through; however, I think it also shows that she just doesn't understand. She's trying to do the things that she knows how to do to be a good mother, and it's just not landing with him.

In the sentence you chose, Mrs. Krebs is referring to the biological mother-son relationship. You've also spoken previously about Harold's religious upbringing. Would you say that, for Harold, those two things—religion and the mother-son dynamic—have radically new definitions after the war?

Absolutely. There's a real breakdown in communication between these two because Mrs. Krebs says, "Don't you love your mother, dear boy," and he says, "No." Then, "His mother looked at him across the table. Her eyes were shiny. She started crying." He says, "I don't love anybody." He's not telling her that he doesn't love *her*. He doesn't love anybody. When he says that, he really means it. She, I think, doesn't understand that. She doesn't understand that something in him has gone away. It hurts her. He realizes that it hurts her, and she's sitting there crying while he's trying to make it up to her. He tries to comfort her. He's kind of going through the motions, but nothing is really real to Krebs. These relationships, they just—if they're complicated, he doesn't want them. The only things he can do are things that he can find the guidance and rules for.

—

"It almost makes you ashamed to feel things."

—

So, he can play pool. He goes off to watch his sister's indoor baseball game. These are things that have set rules. People do the things that they're supposed to do, but anything complicated, like the loving relationship Krebs might have had with his mother before the war or like religion, these things don't mean anything to him anymore. He just can't handle it. He tries to block that out. Mrs. Krebs definitely does not understand that it's not personal.

The other reason Harold goes off to watch his sister's baseball game is that he can't deal with grown women. He sees these beautiful women walking around town. He likes to look at them but can't engage them. They're too complicated. He can look at the patterns of their clothes. This is another thing about this story that I find disturbing: the only women that he can connect with are children and sex workers. He's all right with the French and German girls that he presumably paid for sex during the war. He can also talk to his little sister, and he could tell her that he cares for her and go see her baseball game, but that's because she's a child. Relationships with a reciprocal power dynamic are too much for him.

Being a parent myself, looking at the story from the mother's perspective, I think we do Hemingway a disservice if we don't recognize that he has captured the mother's pain here as well. She's not a villain, she's not an embarrassment, and she's not Grace. She's a mother who is deeply hurt and confused that the son she sent off to war has not returned to her. She has her son back bodily, but she doesn't realize that a part of him is missing.

>·<

VERNA KALE is Associate Editor of the Hemingway Letters Project and co-editor, with Sandra Spanier and Miriam B. Mandel, of Volume 6: *The Letters of Ernest Hemingway, 1934–1936*. She is the author of the critical biography *Ernest Hemingway*, editor of *Teaching Hemingway and Gender*, and author of articles and shorter pieces in the Teaching Hemingway series, the Reading Hemingway series, *The New Hemingway*, *The Hemingway Review*, the *Journal of Popular Culture*, *Hemingway in Context*, and *Ernest Hemingway and the Geography of Memory*.

CRAIG MCDONALD

"Old Newsman Writes: A Letter from Cuba"

What is your one true sentence and why?

This sentence comes from a piece called "Old Newsman Writes: A Letter from Cuba," which Hemingway published in *Esquire*: "All good books are alike in that they are truer than if they had really happened and after you are finished reading one you will feel that all that happened to you and afterwards it all belongs to you; the good and the bad, the ecstasy, the remorse and sorrow, the people and the places and how the weather was."

That sentence appeals to me because it was on a poster in the English lounge when I was a student at Ohio State University. It struck me as at once a Hemingway mission statement but also, for an aspiring writer, something that you couldn't help but aspire to achieve. Also, it speaks to a kind of shadow play. I see a tension in Hemingway's own work between history and memoir, and fact in fiction.

What does the word "truer" mean to you in that context?

I think what he was always trying to dodge was the sense of reportage in fiction. It's a bit like stroking smoke, trying to define what makes something truer, but there is in Hemingway at his finest, something that's sublime and hard to put your hand on. Just through the language and the spareness and the very careful choice of words, you get this sense of reality that goes beyond just simple description.

You said that as a student you were struck by this particular quote. It's almost a pep talk to himself as he's about to approach the blank page. Do you use a similar approach; is it applicable to your writing career?

No, it's one of these things where I always have the first sentence and the last sentence, and then everything in between is a sort of improvisation. You definitely strive for something that seems to have that very authentic opening. In *A Moveable Feast*, he talks about, too, that if he couldn't quite find one true sentence that satisfied him, he would dig deeper down into whatever he was writing until a sentence seized on him as being authentic. And then that would become the opening. He talks about cutting away the scrollwork. I find that in my own work at times. I've written chapters that were easily discarded, and I think famously Fitzgerald was the one who talked Hemingway into knocking out the entire front end of *The Sun Also Rises*, which he thought was overly expository.

Is writing journalism a different sensibility or mentality than writing fiction?

Absolutely. Journalism is extremely perishable and probably even more perishable now than at any other point, because so much of it is being presented online, and you're constantly updating stories online. Kind of cynically, we use a lot of software now, metrically to measure, and can see how far into a story a person reads. It's sort of disheartening to see that even the most complicated and polished piece of journalism you write to an online audience, that's maybe read for something on the order of about one minute. When you sit down to write fiction, I think of the kind of advice that Hemingway would give: start each day and read what you've written to that point and then go on from there to resume your composition and just constantly reread and reread. I don't know how many times I read a manuscript, but it has to be a hundred or more times, and you get to a point where you're just absolutely sick of the book and don't want to read the damn thing again.

When you're rereading one of your own manuscripts, do you find that you are paring down more than you're inserting?

Absolutely. Particularly, for some reason, the older I get, the more I tend to overwrite. So, I do find myself subtracting. Twenty-five, thirty pages can come out of what would be a first complete draft of a book. It's really not paragraphs coming out so much. It's just words here and there to tighten up sentences.

You used the word "authentic," and I want to go back to what we were saying about one true sentence, and how it seems that Hemingway might be using that word. There's the authentic, there's the real, and then there's what happened. He says in *A Moveable Feast*, "It was easy then because there was always one true sentence that I knew or had seen or had heard someone say." But it can't just be true because it happened, right? It has to have that other sort of alchemy that is going to advance the story. How do you parse that?

It's very difficult to parse, particularly in reading Hemingway because he plays so many games. In *Green Hills of Africa*, he says that this is a nonfiction book, but if you want to read it as a novel, you can try and do that. You can insert your own love interest if you care to do that. He's trying to posture that it's a true account of a safari and an experiment to see if it could compete with a work of imagination. And then he sort of reverses that in *A Moveable Feast*, where he says it can be regarded as a work of fiction. Even though it's allegedly a memoir, it can throw some light on what has been written as fact. So, if they don't conform to what really happened, who cares, as long as it reads well and it reaches you as a reader in some way and stays with you.

———

"As a fiction writer, he's a sublime poet.
As a poet, he's a terrible poet."

———

I can read a book and forget what I've read a half hour later with so many authors, but Hemingway does hang in your head in a very powerful way. I think it's that spareness of writing. I mean, he actually started as a poet, and I think he was a really terrible poet, but he is writing through that kind of spareness and choosing of certain words to repeat at strategic points. As a fiction writer, he's a sublime poet. As a poet, he's a terrible poet.

You've taken this mantra of one true sentence and you've made it a motif of your novels. How does this idea become essentially a figure in your work?

Hemingway is a recurring character in several of the books. The protagonist of my books is a contemporary of Hemingway's who came up through pulp writing while he was living in Paris and trying to actually become an artistic fiction writer. The two of them play a game with each other about one true sentence, where one will throw out the beginning of a kind of a hard-boiled fragment sentence, and then it's up to the other to finish it in some pithy way. My character is called by critics "a man who lives what he writes and writes what he lives." That was something that I really picked up from Hemingway, too, because he's constantly confused with his characters.

I actually wrote a book called *One True Sentence*. In fact, in France that translated into *La phrase qui tue*, which is "the sentence that kills." Again, it's just that concept of writing a sentence in a particular way that it endures in the mind of a reader for a very long period of time. In the books, Hemingway actually gifts the protagonist, my character Hector Lassiter, with a Zippo lighter that says, *One true sentence.* So it is a recurring mantra for both of them.

Is there something about reading Hemingway sentence-by-sentence that is particularly rewarding?

Yeah, I tend to read Hemingway aloud to myself just to hear the way the words are put together. That's more of the short stories. When you write a novel, obviously you can't be that distilled and intense across 70,000 or 80,000 words, but in his short fiction, the best of the short fiction, you know, virtually every sentence seems to lay right and have that kind of resonance.

>·<

Craig McDonald is an award-winning journalist, editor, and fiction writer. He is the author of the internationally acclaimed *Hector Lassiter* series of crime novels that features Hemingway as a fictional character. His short fiction has appeared in literary magazines and anthologies.

ANDREW FARAH

ONE TRUE SENTENCE FROM
"Ten Indians"

What is your one true sentence and why?

My sentence is actually the last one from "Ten Indians." In the story, after Nick Adams returns with the Garners from a Fourth of July celebration, his father tells him that Prudence Mitchell, Nick's Native American girlfriend, has cheated on him. Nick's father says he was up "by the Indian camp" and saw her "in the woods with Frank Washburn." Nick is, of course, devastated. But then, "In the morning there was a big wind blowing and the waves were running high up on the beach and he was awake a long time before he remembered that his heart was broken."

This sentence captured my attention even in high school, the sensitivity and sentimentality of it and that connectedness that Hemingway had with that youthful sort of melancholy.

Probably, there's no one more sentimental than a child, right? Hemingway had that connection back to those vulnerable ages, five to nine, when your emotional state was just so transient and critical, and you could decide your heart was broken or you could decide it wasn't. It was sometimes dependent on external events and sometimes not. The sentence is an elegant and beautiful connection to that period of emotional innocence. It just resonated with me.

80% of the sentence is about the weather, and Hemingway doesn't really talk about the heart of the sentence until the very end. Does that satirize a young boy's emotions or not? What is the phenomenon of memory that you wouldn't remember it immediately?

I don't think he's satirizing so much as setting a tone with the weather. I think that at that age, it is more the vulnerability and the ability to be distracted and the transient nature of that emotional state. Of course, it also speaks to Nick's connectedness to the earth and the world around him and to his senses. I think there's a lot of that in this story, like when he walks back from the Garners' home and he's walking back barefoot in the mud. There's a lot of earthiness and rawness in the story.

I had always associated having your heart broken with something that is, or isn't. It wasn't something you had to remember or identify with; however, Hemingway seems to speak to the subjectivity of emotions.

I think he does. You've got to wonder why Nick's heart was broken. It's interesting that people have really questioned the motivations of his dad. What the heck was he doing spying on Nick's little girlfriend, Prudence, anyway? You know, that's all curious. And Nick's cross-examination of his dad is pretty good. His dad is very dismissive. So, there's a little bit of mystery there. It's curious that the original manuscript, the 1925 manuscript, really has no indication of Prudence betraying Nick. He goes to bed happy, but Prudence comes to the window crying, and her family members have come back drunk, and she says she's "never going to kiss anyone again." It's clear that the poor little girl has been sexually assaulted. In 1926, that ending was discarded. The story ends when the dad is sprawled out on the bed saying, "Oh, Christ never let me tell a kid something rotten again," and kicking himself for doing it. Only in the 1927 ending do we get Nick's broken heart, and the manuscript had the alternative title of "A Broken Heart." It's interesting that Hemingway himself tried three different endings, all of which are very profound and all of which are very hurtful in a way.

In that last paragraph, Hemingway says, "after a while he forgot to think about Prudence and finally he went to sleep." Of course, many Hemingway characters have that issue of trying to sleep, trying to forget, trying to deal with a trauma. It's something Hemingway chronicles all the time.

He does, and denial, or rather, forgetting unpleasant things, is useful to our brains. It's useful to our psyche. It's funny that you mentioned the issue of sleep because in another story, "Now I Lay Me," a veteran is just terrified to go to sleep because he thinks his soul will escape him. Hemingway wrote that when he himself came back from World War I, he had to have the light on, or his sister would stay with him, and so forth. There was something going on there with sleep. His World War I experience not only included the mortar blast, but a great deal more horrific sights. No wonder he couldn't sleep very comfortably for a long time. Was that a PTSD symptom? Possibly.

This whole discussion of insomnia, PTSD, and war brings to mind your book *Hemingway's Brain*, where you suggest that Hemingway was actually misdiagnosed and that his own history of concussions—including the World War I mortar injury you just mentioned—played a critical role in his downward spiral.

The book was inspired by a question from Bill Smallwood, who collaborated on Tillie Arnold's book, *The Idaho Hemingway*. He asked why Hemingway had deteriorated and declined after he received shock therapy, or ECT, because Smallwood had read that, generally, ninety percent of patients improve with this treatment. I met Bill just out of residency, and I remembered thinking that the patients who received ECT and declined, rather than improved, had some kind of organic brain disease or, rather, something more neurological, and the ECT was the physiological stressor that propelled or accentuated that neurological decline.

We've heard the bipolar idea. Everybody likes to say Hemingway was bipolar, but I think that's just simply not true. He had a son, Gregory, who was certainly bipolar, but Hemingway himself never had a manic episode.

—

"He had that connection back to those vulnerable ages, five to nine, when your emotional state was just so transient and critical ..."

—

People also like to blame alcohol for a great many things. It was certainly a contributor. By his early fifties, though, Hemingway was showing signs of a form of dementia. Now, dementia is just sort of a blanket term, meaning a cognitive decline involving mental processing, and memory deficits, and can also include mood and behavior changes. The primary sources of these changes for him were all the concussions he had. We're talking about major concussions throughout his lifetime. They caused cumulative damage, and that was the majority of the pathology for him. This is what we now call chronic traumatic encephalopathy (CTE). Combined with all this, there was probably a component of alcohol-associated decline. There was also probably a component of vascular disease of the brain. So, we know that people with one or two large strokes can have a form of dementia, but we also know that patients who have an accumulation of smaller strokes over time can have dementing-type symptoms and illness. For Hemingway, being a poorly controlled hypertensive and pre-diabetic, and possibly diabetic at times, he'd be at risk for that, too. Although it's impossible to fraction out the exact ratio of pathology, I think the majority of this problem was from the concussions.

To help give a better sense of that cumulative damage of concussions, could you describe the kinds of head injuries Hemingway received over the course of his life?

Hemingway might have had some football-associated concussions. He also had a boxing life. He had three bad car wrecks, two plane crashes, and other accidents. One night in 1928, he was out in Paris drinking with Archibald MacLeish, came home and, instead of pulling the cord for the commode, accidentally pulled the cord for the skylight, which fell and hit his head, leaving that famous upside-down horseshoe scar on his forehead. As well, everyone probably knows about his war injury, where the five-gallon Austrian mortar exploded, knocking Hemingway unconscious. That was so quintessential to his life and writing, and he wrote about his out-of-body experience in *A Farewell to Arms*. The important thing about that is that about twenty percent of returning veterans who have suffered these blast-wave injuries report out-of-body experiences. If you think about it, you can have a concussion from a direct blow, and he certainly had his share of those; however, that blast-wave concussion is unique in that the damage it causes is usually in the connectivity between the grey and white brain matter, or the connectivity of the brain cells themselves.

At the end of your book, you provide a retrospective diagnosis of Hemingway. How conclusive can this kind of diagnosis be? What information do you feel confident about, and what information would be helpful to have as you home in on your diagnosis?

That's a great point, because all illness, particularly mental illness, is very much bound by its time and place. You go back over 2,000 years and it's an imbalance of the humors. Go back to fifty A.D., and if somebody has seizures or psychosis, it was considered demonic possession. Then we move forward to the Middle Ages and these illnesses are attributed to witchcraft. By the early 1700s, it's something akin to "moral insanity." Only by around 1850 do we start having modern, or almost modern, language to describe these kinds of things. So, Hemingway is in modern times, right? He's a twentieth-century guy. I think, too, we have extensive biographies, memoirs from people who were close to him, thousands and thousands of his own letters. We even have an FBI file on this patient. There's no shortage of data. Many of us own Brewster Chamberlin's *The Hemingway Log*, which documents what he was doing nearly every day of his life. I can't think of a literary life more extensively biographied or studied. The fact is, if I interviewed him, I think it would just confirm what I know. I don't mean to sound too arrogant about it, but I don't think there is any doubt what he was suffering from.

➤·◄

ANDREW FARAH is a forensic psychiatrist who has been a medical director at the University of North Carolina and Wake Forest hospitals, served as Associate Residency Director at Cone Health in Greensboro, NC, and now focuses on geriatric psychiatry at Novant Health. His book, *Hemingway's Brain*, was published in 2017 by University of South Carolina Press. He is now completing a psychiatric biography of Ezra Pound.

JOSHUA FERRIS

What is your one true sentence and why?

My one true sentence is the concluding line to *The Sun Also Rises*. It may be Hemingway's most famous sentence: "Isn't it pretty to think so?" Jake Barnes says it to Lady Brett Ashley at the end of the book as a reflection on the romance between the two that will never come to be. It's the perfect line for many reasons. It's beautiful. It's romantic. It's heartbreaking. It has that wonderful word choice—"pretty"—which perhaps no one else would think to use. It's ambiguous. It's ironic. Most impressive, perhaps, is that it consists of six short words. It's the sort of line that every writer dreams of coming up with and putting at the end of his or her book and just sort of sitting back and going, "I did it. I did it. I did it well." I love it. It's perfect.

When you say writers dream of writing this kind of concluding line, what's the theory behind endings to novels or short stories? What do you shoot for? Is it a resolution or is it ambiguity? Is it something different?

Perhaps it is all of those things: something that concludes with a certain amount of resolution, but that paradoxically rings with ambiguity, the ambiguity that is real life. The writer has found a way to discourage dishonesty from sneaking in at the last moment, which can really clobber a book. The sort of dishonesty that wants to wrap things up in a tidy bow, or convey a feeling that hasn't been described. You can make it through a good deal of a book and love it and come to some kind of false note at the end and really be disappointed. It might not even be outright dishonest. It might simply lack the kind of vitality that had been so present in the previous pages. It turns a reader off. And the reader who is sold, who is all in, arrives at the end only to find this fraudulent note lying in wait. Hemingway's ending is the antidote to all those things. It crystalizes. It distills. It revivifies. It continues the life of the book. I mean, it's so good, you practically need to start over again immediately.

In writing your novels, did you know what the last line was going to be before you wrote it?

Then We Came to the End was meant to conclude differently—in fact, with maybe another twenty pages or so. A coda about one of the characters during a very intense night of his life. That would parallel an earlier occasion in that book in which I followed the female boss around in a similar way, and I liked the symmetry of that. But when I reached the end, I realized I couldn't have that coda. It diminished the line that came before, which was the perfect line with which to end the book, and so I had to adapt. I had to adjust. No more coda. I'd written the line I needed. That line resonates with me even now— or, I should say, I don't loathe it. Which, you know, is never a guarantee. So, I cut those twenty pages away and learned a lesson in adaptability. Also, in efficiency. How to give less so that the reader gets more. Which was always Hemingway's genius.

That line just ends with Jake's voice, but Hemingway doesn't tell you how he says it. It's really incumbent upon the reader to supply his or her own specificity. How do you hear that last sentence?

Well, it's the right question to ask. It's the question that really gets at the heart of what makes the line so great. It's full of honest feeling and it's intended to be genuinely moving both to the reader and to Brett. Jake doesn't like to talk about his feelings. He doesn't like to think his thoughts. He's an elusive man who nevertheless does let us in from time to time, and when he lets us in, he becomes something more than the other characters in the book. His little insights and his vulnerabilities provide the engine of emotion that keeps us so attached to him and to his story. Because the story isn't just one of bullfighting and drinking wine. It's all about damage and suffering and romantic agony. Here, at last, he's really, in an artful and somewhat studied or mannered way, nevertheless conceding to Brett that he loves her and that the great tragedy of their lives is their inability to be together. I should say that that line is eternally adaptable, too, just incredibly applicable to all sorts of situations. When that line lands, you want to steal it for yourself and apply it to all of the tragic situations in your own life. For about a hundred years now that line has taken on a life of its own because it is the perfect vehicle to convey all sorts of disappointments and disillusionments that we might experience at any given moment, whether romantic or professional, or personal, or psychological, or whatever the case may be.

—

"Hemingway's ending... It crystalizes. It distills.
It revivifies. It continues the life of the book.
I mean, it's so good, you practically need
to start over again immediately."

—

If you had to defile that sentence by adding an adverb to show how Jake says it, it would be, maybe, "wistfully"?

"Heartbreakingly"? "Guttingly"? It would have to be something more than "wistful" because it really does feel like the sentence is obscuring a tremendous amount of emotion in the way that most of those conversations that happen—especially among men—in the book obscure enormous amounts of emotion, vulnerability, and weakness.

I wonder if you could speak, as a writer, about this balance between omission and explication.

To some extent you can think of a short story or a novel—a good one, a successful one—as being the most elegant and efficient conveyor of information vital to the human condition. What that means, really, is that you, as the writer, don't want to repeat on page ten what you've put down on page one. You certainly don't want to put it down a third time on page twelve. The writing has to be concise, first and foremost. That concision is at odds to some extent with the writer's motivation, what drove him or her to the desk to begin with, which is to get some point across, to leave an impression, to reveal something important. Maybe it's the memorialization of some lost love or some aspect of life, what's important to that writer or what's heartbreaking or what's enraging ... any number of things. Hemingway demonstrates the vitality of leaving it all out. It's a kind of negative vitality. I would love to do more of it in my work, but I'm not very good at it. I seem to overwrite every damn thing, then spend too much time revising things out.

As a reader, are you drawn to the aesthetic of a writer who shares and is abundant or somebody like Hemingway, who is more spare?

Very much the former until I see it done by the latter. The former, if you can do it with aplomb, with real elegance and beauty, the way that, say, Vladimir Nabokov does it—I think that, for whatever reason, aligns best with my particular aesthetic. When that maximalist writing is done poorly, it's even worse than bad Hemingway. You can read bad Hemingway very easily at bed at night and not throw the book across the room. If you're reading somebody that's going on and on, especially in that postmodern manner in which it all just seems to be masturbatory play, you want to hurl the book across the room and out the window and then leave the house and set it on fire.

In juxtaposing those two sensibilities, it seems like ending a novel with a spare quote like "Isn't it pretty to think so?" is a courageous act where a writer or any artist gives the reader only so much. Do you ever find that, as a writer, you're trusting the reader to pick up on things that you don't want to explicitly state?

Oh, it's enormously courageous. It's very trusting of the reader. Eventually, I get there. I edit enough that, hopefully, there's something left to the reader to interpret. That interpretive task, especially with a good reader, is constantly going on anyway. Throw that good reader a morsel and she will take it and digest it in the five or six ways that it might be turned over, and there's a lot of satisfaction to be had in that. It's an enormous act of faith, especially in Hemingway's time. By this point, anyone who had made a splash in American fiction had been more on the maximal side. Nathaniel Hawthorne, Henry James, Edith Wharton, Herman Melville—these are maximalists, and their books were considered illustrious examples of how to write good fiction. Then along comes Hemingway, who sums up so many of the feelings that might have occurred in *The Portrait of a Lady* in just six words. It's really, really courageous; it breaks the mold after that because it's just so ballsy that nobody knows where to even go from there. Even Hemingway had a hard time repeating that success because it's incredibly hard to do. Your task as a writer seems to be to ram some point about love or life or disillusionment or betrayal down the reader's throat, and here's this guy, this genius who just merely suggests. He just knows intuitively in his bones, that was how it should be done. Writers like that come into the world with that gift. They're born with that trust.

✦•◄

JOSHUA FERRIS is the best-selling author of four novels and a collection of short stories, *The Dinner Party*. He has been a finalist for the National Book Award, winner of the Barnes & Noble Discover Award, and the winner of the 2008 PEN/Hemingway Award for his novel *Then We Came to the End*. He was shortlisted for the Man Booker Prize and won the International Dylan Thomas Prize for his third novel, *To Rise Again at a Decent Hour*. His fourth novel, *A Calling for Charlie Barnes*, was published in 2021 to critical acclaim.

ROSS K. TANGEDAL

ONE TRUE SENTENCE FROM
"Indian Camp"

What is your one true sentence and why?

My one true sentence is from "Indian Camp" and it's not very lyrical, but it's very Hemingway: "It all took a long time."

What is the context for that sentence and why does that jump out at you?

At this point in the story Nick and his father are in the Indian camp and his father has begun the operation on the Indian woman and it has already become a traumatic experience for Nick. He's been bombarded by his senses, what he sees and hears and smells. At this point, I argue, his eyes are closed as he's holding the basin for his father. I don't believe Nick sees the surgery—his eyes are closed—but he hears everything, and he has no way of describing what he hears. So, we get a very innocent and juvenile sentence, "It all took a long time."

"It" could be any number of things. Hemingway is so good with impersonal pronouns across his fiction. The readers need to provide what "it" refers to because someone of Nick's age—he's somewhere between ten and twelve—doesn't know what any of this is. He has no experience with surgery or with the way the woman is screaming, the cutting of flesh. That "it" doesn't mean labor, it doesn't mean childbirth, it doesn't mean surgery. It's just the multi-sensory trauma that occurs all around him. Nick has no way of understanding, so the only way it can be described to the reader is, "It all took a long time."

Does that understatement and lack of specificity somehow become more powerful? Is that typical of Hemingway's approach to these types of traumatic experiences?

Absolutely. Especially in these early stories. And "Up in Michigan" is a really good example of Hemingway's use of "it." When Jim is assaulting Liz at the end of the story, it reads: "She had to have it but it frightened her." So, yet again, the use of the impersonal pronoun is used to get the reader involved in the trauma, because now the reader has to supply the "it"—there is no definite definition of the "it"—so if the reader is able to construct these traumatic experiences, to describe the darkness, his use of "it" is the perfect word to help us get to the darkness in Hemingway.

When you teach "Up in Michigan," is there ambiguity in Jim's aggressiveness and Liz's reaction? Has Hemingway left that open, or do you think that the text is coaching us one way or the other?

Almost every single time we all come to the conclusion that clearly Jim raped Liz. That conclusion is there, but it's also the way that Hemingway brings us to that dark moment and how Liz has all of these different reactions to what's going on.

———

"His use of 'it' is the perfect word to help us get to the darkness in Hemingway."

———

One of the difficult things we talk about, for instance, is when she clearly feels the pleasure of the sexual moment, while also feeling the pain of it. She doesn't want it, but she feels like she wants it. It so clearly helps us understand the issues of consent today, the notion of consent, and what it means. Just because Liz may have enjoyed parts of their sexual encounter does not mean that she wasn't raped.

We have conversations about why Hemingway sets up this rape scene earlier with several paragraphs of Liz's sexual awakening—Liz masturbating to thoughts of Jim in her bed; Liz looking at Jim from far away and looking at his arms and the hair on his arms; Liz literally falling in love with him in a very juvenile, childish, innocent way. But that innocence is colliding with a sexual awakening. And then to have both of those moments of innocence taken away by Jim, who is the aggressor, who is the adult in this situation—it makes for great conversation, which is why I teach it.

The point that I think is particularly Hemingwayesque is at the end: "There was a mist coming up from the bay ..." And then there's a whole bunch of other stuff, but the last sentence is "A *cold* mist was coming up through the woods from the bay." So, even that little addition of "cold" shows the variation in the repetition that gives it the meaning. What a wonderful last sentence.

Oh, I think so. This plays right into "Indian Camp" and the canoes going across the water early in the morning, and the mist on the top of the water. His Michigan stories are full of that imagery. There's ominousness, too, in that a lot of my students say, well, she's going to get pregnant. And if that's the case, if the ominous nature is that she's returning up the dock back to the Smiths' house, she will be ostracized from this community, this very small community that only has four homes and four families. Who got her pregnant? Will she say? Will she have a bastard child? Jim will certainly not take responsibility for a child. So, yes, the cold mist could mean any number of things, but clearly it also means that she may very well be pregnant completely lose her stature in the community as a young girl.

I always like to talk about the darkness in Hemingway, and that word is really important—*darkness*. Michael Reynolds talked about that in one of his biographies, about the darkness in Michigan. Michigan represents the sort of dark moments for Hemingway that he then turns into fiction.

There's also this striking sequence: "Liz liked Jim very much. She liked it the way he walked over from the shop and often went to the kitchen door to watch for him to start down the road. She liked it about his mustache. She liked it about how white his teeth were when he smiled. She liked it very much that he didn't look like a blacksmith. She liked it how much D.J. Smith and Mrs. Smith liked Jim. One day she found that she liked it the way the hair was black on his arms and how white they were above the tanned line when he washed up in the washbasin outside the house. Liking that made her feel funny." This sort of repetition, similar to one we'll also see in "Soldier's Home," is conspicuous. Is this Gertrude Stein's influence?

Sure. Well, that's paragraph three. That's *the paragraph* of "Up in Michigan" before you get to the end. Where it says: "Liz likes Jim," and "like" is just such a Hemingway word. My students and I, we unpack that for a long time. What does it mean that Liz "likes" Jim?

I think it's clear that the repetitive nature of the story is very Steinian, and that's a good thing. And maybe—and Hemingway would probably argue that as well—that's why she didn't like it. He was kind of coming up on that Stein influence, but still that repetition is very clearly a Steinian influence while, at the same time marrying the idea of Sherwood Anderson's communities. *Winesburg, Ohio* is about a small town; Horton Bay, Michigan, that's a small rural area that Hemingway is clearly trying to investigate.

When I come across that famous passage with the repetitions in "Soldier's Home," I say, well, that is such a beautiful description of a traumatized, shellshocked veteran. But it's a different argument for why that type of phrasing and repetition would apply to Liz in this particular situation. I wonder why Hemingway opted for such a conspicuous style here?

I think it's because he's hinting at her age and the inability for someone who is as young as she is to make complex statements about her feelings, especially sexual feelings that she has never felt before. That is why this story is so important. Not only does he have a female protagonist, but he has a very young female protagonist who is having a sexual awakening without any understanding of what sex is, what it becomes, what it could be.

That repetition signals her age, which Hemingway was so good at, especially in *In Our Time* with stories like "Indian Camp" and "The End of Something," helping us understand Nick Adams's age at different points. I think he's practicing it in "Up in Michigan" with the very young Liz Coates.

➤·◄

Ross K. Tangedal is Assistant Professor of English and Director of the Cornerstone Press at the University of Wisconsin–Stevens Point. He is the author of *The Preface: American Authorship in the Twentieth Century* and co-editor of *Editing the Harlem Renaissance*. He is a contributing editor for the NEH-funded Hemingway Letters Project, where he is associate editor of Volume 6: *The Letters of Ernest Hemingway, 1934–1936*.

SUZANNE DEL GIZZO

"Big Two-Hearted River"

What is your one true sentence and why?

My sentence is "He was in his home where he had made it." "Big Two-Hearted River" is a story about a camping and fishing trip. Nick Adams is alone on this trip. As context for the sentence, he's setting up his campsite after a long day of hiking to it, and Hemingway writes, "He had not been unhappy all day. This was different though. Now things were done. There had been this to do. Now it was done. It had been a hard trip. He was very tired. That was done. He had made his camp. He was settled. Nothing could touch him. It was a good place to camp. He was there, in the good place. He was in his home where he had made it. Now he was hungry."

I just love the simple, short, staccato nature of the sentences. I'm a list keeper. I actually rewrite lists sometimes just to cross things off. These sentences have that feeling to me, where Nick's sort of ticking through the things that he had to do. He's really present in the moment where he can relax. This is a great story because it contains both vulnerability and resiliency. Nick is struggling to anchor himself in the world. Creating your own home, even if it's a campsite or a tent is a huge accomplishment for Nick in the end. That peace it gives him is an incredible experience for the reader to witness.

The sentence before your one true sentence is "He was there, in the good place." What does that mean?

I assume it's not a reference to the TV show that my daughter loves now! I think it's a psychological state more than it is just an actual location. Here, Nick is very much in his body. He's being very present in his body and trying to physically exhaust himself. It's a feeling of presence in the moment, in the body, anchored in the world, and that kind of deep orientation is unusual.

"Home" is a big deal with Hemingway. It's hard to talk about this story without thinking about the story "Soldier's Home," where Krebs, a different character, returns to his hometown and doesn't feel at home at all. I don't know that Hemingway ever felt tremendously happy in his home life, but after returning from World War I he certainly felt even more alienated. The values of his parents weren't his values. They didn't live a life the way that he liked to live a life, and so he felt very much at sea.

If we think about Hemingway's largely itinerant life as part of the Lost Generation, "home" was an important concept for him, but it didn't refer to a place. It referred to a state of mind or a state of connection to others.

It makes it even more striking that he's referring to his campsite as his home. You can call it the place you'll sleep for the night, but your home—

Right! It's all about, I think, this recognition that the traditional identity markers—where you're from, your nationality—those things didn't matter as much to Hemingway. He really wanted to create himself. And he did. That's a little bit about what this story means: making yourself comfortable in yourself, being comfortable in the world. So, to my mind, that agency is both an incredible burden and also an incredible experience; it's a privilege to be able to make yourself that way. Here, he is starting to feel his independent, adult life, separate from the things that had defined him. He now feels able to create himself in the world, which is incredible.

The sentence that ends the paragraph you're quoting from is "Now he was hungry." It seems like when people talk about hunger in Hemingway, they're talking about desire and creativity, right? In *A Moveable Feast*, there's "hunger-thinking." In "Big Two-Hearted River," is it just being hungry because you're in tune to your physical exhaustion or is there more to it?

I know what you mean. Most of the time in Hemingway, hunger was a good discipline. It is connected to his ability to write well or to be inspired. In this story though, at the very beginning, he says that he left it all behind, including the need to write. I actually believe that this is a more elemental, more straightforward hunger, that these are much more physical markers. This story, unlike, the *Moveable Feast* reference, is really about somebody trying to hold it together and finding a way to self-soothe. There's that famous idea that this is a story about the war with no mention of the war in it. Maybe the burned over town and the black grasshoppers are somehow a metaphor for the damage that the war has done, like Nick feels contaminated, as if he's been changed by the war. But now he's in nature and "the river was there" and he's trying to find a way to self-soothe and hold on to it.

—

"This is a great story because it contains both vulnerability and resiliency."

—

What I love about this piece is that it's so ritualistic. All those pages about making coffee and the right way to touch a fish. It's all about rituals. When you start to realize that he's so focused on the rituals as a way of connecting to the world again, after what I guess we presume is an upsetting experience, if not a trauma of war, the tenuousness of our connection to ourselves and to our world feels so alive to me in this story. He's clinging to these rituals. They're structuring his life in a way that allows him to recover.

Do you read "Big Two-Hearted River" as a positive story? An affirmative one?

I read it as a human one. He doesn't fish the swamp. He has real limits in the story. I don't think we can say that he's recovered or that he's well. He's trying to recover. He's working on it. That's maybe another reason that I really respond to the story. It accepts the fact that it's a process. It doesn't depict an easy optimism. It also doesn't feel particularly sinister either, the way that something like his story "Now I Lay Me" does. It does feel as if he's just settling down into the process.

Suzanne, the passage you chose seems like the kind of prose that, when people want to either make fun of Hemingway or satirize him or call his writing "Hemingwayesque," they point to these really short, direct, punctuation-less sentences. How common is this kind of sequence in all of Hemingway? Or is it an outlier?

I actually think it's more of an outlier. Justin Rice at LitCharts has done some studies of Hemingway's prose. Using data analysis, his studies seem to bear out what I suspect, which is that Hemingway's style is not quite as short or as terse as most people come away thinking that it is. Maybe those passages are particularly memorable, but I don't think they're as common in his writing as a lot of people think. I would also say that when people make fun of Hemingway and they write the short staccato sentences, the reason why it doesn't work is because they are not working with the omitted thing.

These sentences from "Big Two-Hearted River" have earned their place on the page because we have a sense of the stress that Nick is under. He actually carries a backpack that's really heavy, so he needs to use a tumpline on his forehead, and he thinks about how heavy the pack is. That, of course, is a metaphor for all that he's carrying emotionally. Those sentences are earned and, when you get to them, they are delivered in a way that you feel the relief of finishing these tasks. It's really funny when people try to make fun of Hemingway because you think, "On how many levels do you not get it?"

➤·◄

SUZANNE DEL GIZZO is Professor of English at Chestnut Hill College and Editor of *The Hemingway Review*. She has published numerous articles in scholarly journals and co-edited three books, most recently *The New Hemingway Studies* (with Kirk Curnutt).

KAWAI STRONG WASHBURN

ONE TRUE SENTENCE FROM

"A Clean, Well-Lighted Place"

What is your one true sentence and why?

The sentence that I selected is near the end of "A Clean, Well-Lighted Place." This story takes place almost entirely in a café at the end of the night, with two waiters and a single customer, an old, deaf man. Most of the story is one long scene, where the two waiters discuss the old man and, finally, try to get him to leave the café. When that scene is over, after the café is closed up, the older waiter leaves and stops at another café to have a drink of his own and mull over thoughts that have sprung up as a result of the encounter with the old man. While he's there, in his head he's thinking—and that's where this particular sentence comes from—"Some lived in it and never felt it but he knew it all was *nada y pues nada y nada y pues nada.*"

Why does that sentence jump out at you?

I think writers always strive for some level of veracity, right? You want what's happening on the page to speak to some bigger truth, something you can't just get from reading facts and figures or things like that. I think that's one of the things people really enjoy about literature, when somebody describes a feeling or a thought or something in a way you've never seen or felt it before. It somehow illuminates and enriches your understanding of the world and the human experience and all those sorts of things.

When Hemingway says "one true sentence," the "true" part of it is speaking to that, the writer's ability to take some bigger, unnameable, or unknowable thing and render it in language in such a way that it feels true. And it feels true in a way that nobody has ever said it that way before, and now the reader understands this thing differently than they did before.

That's why I selected the specific sentence I did from "A Clean, Well-Lighted Place." That sentence contains the entire story in it. When those two waiters are discussing the old man, they aren't *really* talking about the old man. They're talking about the entire arc of a human life. The older waiter believes he understands the old man in a way the younger waiter doesn't. Their discussion is one of youth versus age, brashness versus experience, hope and optimism versus an ambivalence about the world. For the older waiter, the things he has experienced in his life boil down to "nada"—it was all *"nada y pues nada."* He believes he has a better understanding of the world than most people—"some lived in it and never felt it"—and this nothingness is at the core of it.

In the sentence you chose, Hemingway uses the word "it" three times: "lived in it," "never felt it," "but he knew it." Hemingway is particularly masterful at using that word, especially where "it" is ambiguous but still powerful. What do you think the "it" is referring to in the sentence?

That's the thing that's beautiful. I think that you can read this a variety of different ways. I can never exactly land on what I think "it" is because this is one of those stories where I keep rereading it and never understand exactly what it is that it does to me. When I first read this story, in my twenties, I had some experience and understanding of death and grief. I was also at a stage in my life where I was starting to ask bigger, existential questions. One of the things that made this story particularly resonant for me is, at the very end of the story, the narrator goes home and he tries to go to sleep. It's been alluded to earlier in the story that there are issues with insomnia and things like that. The narrator refers to himself as being among the people that need a light to help them get to sleep, to help them get to that point where they're at peace. So, I think that the "it" that he's talking about here is the same "it" that keeps him up at night, that makes him unable to sleep.

—

"He believes he has a better understanding of the world than most people—'some lived in it and never felt it'— and this nothingness is at the core of it."

—

When I think about "it" in this story, I feel like it has to do with death, with what happens after we die, with God, or whatever things are that are bigger, that are outside of us. My reading of the story is that, in these sorts of moments when he's at the café at the end of the night, when everybody else has gone and it's quiet and the lights are still on, the narrator believes that he has some understanding of the great beyond or what the meaning is of what comes after this. There's some peace he gets from that. That allows him to be more at peace with the idea that maybe nothing happens. After we die, maybe there's nothing. Maybe all of this means absolutely nothing, and we die and everything else is just meaningless.

It's also only a three- or four-page story. I wonder how you react to somebody who writes such a profound story in so few words. It must be quite a feat.

It's the hardest thing to achieve as a writer, and definitely something to aspire to. Truly good short stories—timeless, classic stories, the sort that go on to be anthologized in literature classes and the canon as a whole—are exceptionally hard to write. It's unfortunate that so many people think, because of the length, that a short story is easier to write. They are significantly harder. In a short story, everything must be distilled to its very essence. Honestly, I probably write novels because I'm so terrible at writing short stories.

>-·-<

KAWAI STRONG WASHBURN was born and raised on the Hamakua coast of the Big Island of Hawai'i. His first novel, *Sharks in the Time of Saviors* won the 2021 PEN/Hemingway Award and the 2021 Minnesota Book Award. It was also longlisted for the 2020 Center for Fiction First Novel Prize and was a finalist for the 2021 PEN/Jean Stein Book Award. President Barack Obama chose it as a favorite novel of 2020, and it was selected as a notable or best book of the year by over a dozen publications, including the *New York Times* and *Boston Globe*.

SCOTT DONALDSON

ONE TRUE SENTENCE FROM
A Farewell to Arms

What is your one true sentence and why?

I came up with the opening sentence from *A Farewell to Arms*, which reads, "In the late summer of that year we lived in a house in a village that looked across the river and the plain to the mountains." Okay, what the heck is distinct about that? What year was it? Where was the house? Where was the village? What was the river? Where was the plain? What were the mountains? We're drawn in.

Hemingway's assuming the reader knows these things; or if you don't know them, you're going to know them pretty soon. He doesn't have to tell us where the house is or what the mountains are or what kind of crops grow there, any of those kinds of details.

This sentence seems a fitting example of Hemingway's iceberg principle. What is that theory?

Well, there are several versions we encounter in his work. Probably the best known one and the most reliable takes place in his book *Death in the Afternoon*. Oddly, the iceberg comes up in the context of Hemingway's diatribe against other writers he thinks are pretentious or trying to show off for the reader. Let me read this to you: "If a writer of prose knows enough about what he is writing about he may omit things that he knows and the reader, if the writer is writing truly enough, will have a feeling of those things as strongly as though the writer had stated them." That is to say, you don't have to say it if you show it. "The dignity of movement of an ice-berg is due to only one-eighth of it being above water. A writer who omits things because he does not know them only makes hollow places in his writing. A writer who appreciates the seriousness of writing so little that he is anxious to make people see he is formally educated, cultured or well-bred is merely a popinjay. And this too remember; a serious writer is not to be confounded with a solemn writer." So, he puts this all in the context of being overly solemn, overly self-important, overly pretentious, which I hadn't really realized until I reread it.

The other major description of the iceberg theory is in *The Paris Review* interview with George Plimpton, but I think we've covered the ground for what the iceberg theory is.

In that passage that you quoted, Hemingway begins, "If a writer of prose knows enough about what he is writing about he may omit things." What is the benefit to a writer in omitting things?

Well, the benefit is the reader's, it seems to me. One of the joys of reading Hemingway is discovering what is meant without being said. When that happens, it gives you a kind of thrill because, in effect, he's putting the reader on an equivalency with him, saying, "You and I know these things. We don't have to say them out loud."

Hemingway seems to refer to it as *his* theory, as if he had invented it. In the mid-1920s and the 1930s, was such a theory of writing prevalent or was it really revolutionary?

Hemingway didn't invent the idea, at least I assume he didn't invent it. He didn't invent the cultural dictum of Ezra Pound's imagism that less is more, which showed up in the writing, music, and architecture of the time. This is something that Hemingway learned from Pound and others, that the best kind of writing is the least showy and the most objective, or most apparently objective writing, with all that objectivity having a subjective component.

—

"One of the joys of reading Hemingway is discovering
what is meant without being said."

—

I'm also thinking of another modernist writer, Willa Cather, whose essay "The Novel Démeublé" describes an approach to unfurnished writing quite similar to Hemingway. What about writers like William Faulkner and James Joyce? Is it simplistic to think of them as anti-iceberg, or did they have a different version of this technique?

Faulkner's an interesting case because he does seem to be long-winded and elaborate in his diction and syntax as opposed to the apparent simplicity of Hemingway's prose. I hesitate to speculate, but I'm sure the concert between a writer and reader extends to a lot of other writers who write much more elaborate prose but still leave things to be discovered.

What you're describing is fascinating. It makes me wonder if the iceberg principle exists on a conceptual basis or a structural basis or even a sentence-by-sentence basis. Even if you write in a more elaborate, complicated prose style, you can still employ a version of the iceberg principle.

I think that's true. So, it isn't simply the apparent surface style that counts, although that certainly counts for Hemingway and is very important for the appreciation and understanding of Hemingway. But I don't think it rules out other kinds of writers enabling their readers to participate in discovering what they're saying.

In trying to discern how revolutionary the iceberg principle was, could you read Shakespeare or the Bible and find the iceberg principle?

I guess I'm on the side of the writers from the Bible who are able to communicate to us in that kind of way, even though they weren't identifying it as a particular theory. I think the idea that Cather is able to speak to a certain kind of audience in the way that they understand, it's useful. And I think Hemingway's speaking to a kind of audience that, if they don't necessarily welcome it, will understand and learn to welcome what he's doing.

It's striking to me that Hemingway seems aware there's a way to do the iceberg incorrectly. He seems to acknowledge the risk of trusting the tip of the iceberg. How do you see that inherent risk in suggestion and implication as opposed to coming right out and saying it?

I think it's a huge risk. Hemingway's short story "Out of Season" is used as an example of the iceberg theory, how he left out the fact that Peduzzi, the drunken fishing guide the Americans had in Cortina d'Ampezzo, had so embarrassed himself that he eventually kills himself. Well, that's not in the story, but Peduzzi is damned embarrassing. You know, you could see how he's making a fool of himself, not only to the American and his wife but to the whole town. He must have seen that.

Do we need to be told that Peduzzi subsequently committed suicide? Or can the story be effectively read without that knowledge?

Oh, yes. Showing the suicide would have overdramatized the story. And it's all there anyway.

➤·◀

SCOTT DONALDSON was one of the nation's leading literary biographers. Among his many biographies are *Hemingway vs. Fitzgerald: The Rise and Fall of a Literary Friendship*, *Fitzgerald & Hemingway: Works and Days*, and the classic *By Force of Will: The Life and Art of Ernest Hemingway*. His *The Paris Husband: How It Really Was Between Ernest and Hadley Hemingway* was published in 2018. He died in 2020 at the age of 92.

RUSSELL BANKS

A Moveable Feast

What is your one true sentence and why?

I've read *A Moveable Feast* at least three times, at different moments in my life. When it was first published in 1964, I was twenty-four years old. I read it again probably in my middle forties. And I read it again just about a month ago. It's a different book each time. It's become a better, kinder, gentler, more forgiving, more guilt-ridden book as I've gotten older.

This is a beautiful sentence to me: "The leaves lay sodden in the rain and the wind drove the rain against the big green autobus at the terminal and the Café des Amateurs was crowded and the windows misted over from the heat and the smoke inside."

The sentence is like a Scorsese tracking shot, where it starts in the window of that little flat over the saw mill, where the leaves let you feel he's looking out the window ("leaves lay sodden in the rain"). Then he moves outside the window ("against the big green autobus"). Then we move down the street a little ways to the café, but we're still outside. Then we move inside ("the Café ... was crowded"), and we see the windows "misted over" from inside, from the heat and the smoke inside. You can't imagine that room now without imagining a crowd of people smoking, standing close to one another, the heat off their bodies, and the smoke of their cigarettes. It's just a fabulous, physical sentence that follows the eye and also follows the sequence of memory from that little flat down to the street and into the café.

What strikes me about hearing you read the sentence is that we have the word "and" over and over, and we don't have any punctuation.

Right. One thing leads to another directly and is absorbed by the other as a result of there being no commas and just being linked by "and." It becomes a coherent and inclusive experience. You simultaneously experience everything going on in that world, in that moment in that world. It's a brilliant sentence. I can't say that it's superior in one way or another to hundreds or thousands of other sentences Hemingway wrote, but for me, personally, it's both beautiful and instructive. That's one reason why so many writers have imitated him for so long and have had to learn how not to imitate him.

Does Hemingway's "one true sentence" approach have any applicability to you as a writer?

Yes, it does. After all, if you write one sentence that's true, you've eliminated at least half of the untold numbers of alternatives where you could go for a second. And writing fiction is a way of eliminating alternatives, until you get to the end where you've only got a few alternatives available to you: either he lives or he dies, or she lives or she dies, or they get married, or they part from one another, and so forth. At the beginning, though, you've got these millions of alternatives. So, you write one sentence, and it creates the next, and the two together then create the third. I think that's what Hemingway's pointing out, and it's true.

I know a lot of writers who follow it, none probably quite as assiduously as he. Although, I'm thinking of Michael Ondaatje, who once told me that he works that way. He writes one sentence and won't write the next until he's satisfied with that one. I think most of us plunge ahead and then go back and fix it later, but Ondaatje is unusual that way.

Russell, you mentioned reading *A Moveable Feast* when it was first published posthumously in 1964. What was Hemingway's presence like for you as a young writer?

It was enormous. He was a figure through which one tried to define and imagine oneself. I was born in 1940 and started writing seriously when I was about eighteen. He was very much alive and very much a figure then, both as a celebrity and as a literary model. I dropped out at the age of 18 and headed south, ending up out there on the Florida Keys in 1961, actually. So, I was very conscious of him as a kind of ghostly presence in my life, which was at that time very attached to and continues to be very attached to south Florida, the Keys, the Caribbean, and so on. Then years later I went to Cuba and visited the Finca Vigía, following in Hemingway's tracks.

—

"With Hemingway, you see everything."

—

There are very few writers one does that for. It's an homage. A pilgrimage. I certainly think that he imprinted so deeply on me that, even as recently as two years ago, I went back to Cuba and went out to the house and walked around. I was with my publisher, Dan Halpern, and he and I were allowed to go through the house. It really was a bit of a shrine to me, I must confess. He really was that important.

What made you gravitate towards Hemingway?

Simply the prose, the short stories more than the novels. I wanted to write short stories—and still do—that had the kind of impact that his had on me. They clarified my mind and they clarified my morality in a way that no other work did. The other writer of that stature and of that presence, really, back then and still to some degree, was William Faulkner. They couldn't be less alike as writers. Reading them, they clarify your mind in a way that no other writers do, at least not for me. Maybe the great nineteenth-century Russians, but that's about it.

The sentence you chose really demonstrates Hemingway's sharp observational skills, doesn't it?

It's interesting to read Hemingway side-by-side with Faulkner, because with Faulkner the visual details don't exist. There are details, abundantly, but they're not visual. You don't see what Faulkner is describing. You may hear it and react to the language, but you don't see it. With Hemingway, you see everything. I first clarified that for myself, not through Hemingway, but through Joseph Conrad. Conrad said his aim was "to make you see." He didn't mean "understand" but "visualize." I began to realize early on that that's key. That's absolutely central. For me as a writer, if I can't see it myself, how can I expect my reader to see it? And then, for me as a reader, I need and want to see it. Hemingway makes that easy. Take the sentence that I read at the beginning; you see that scene because he saw it as he wrote it.

Do these visual details need to be grounded in observational authenticity? In other words, does the writer need to have actually seen it, or can it be true in the imagination?

For some writers, it has to be literally seen or experienced in reality because their visual imagination is not easily stimulated. In my own case, I don't feel that I depend upon visible reality in order to write a sentence that has some truth to it. But as soon as I start writing, I start visualizing. I think that was true for Hemingway, too. I mean, he was not necessarily reporting, literally, everything that he set down in fiction. He was careful to say at the beginning of *A Moveable Feast* that it really should be considered a work of fiction. When he was remembering Paris and writing about it forty years later, that was something he was imagining. Memory is an act of the imagination. For him, his visual imagination most of all.

➤·◄

RUSSELL BANKS has been a PEN/Faulkner finalist and was twice a finalist for the Pulitzer Prize, for his novels *Continental Drift* and *Cloudsplitter*. He is also the author of many other works of fiction, including *Affliction, Rule of the Bone,* and *Foregone.*

GAIL SINCLAIR

ONE TRUE SENTENCE FROM
A Farewell to Arms

What is your one true sentence and why?

The one I chose comes from the opening chapter of *A Farewell to Arms*: "There were mists over the river and clouds on the mountain and the trucks splashed mud on the road and the troops were muddy and wet in their capes; their rifles were wet and under their capes the two leather cartridge-boxes on the front of the belts, gray leather boxes heavy with the packs of clips of thin, long 6.5 mm. cartridges, bulged forward under the capes so that the men, passing on the road, marched as though they were six months gone with child."

That's tremendous. Why does this moment stand out?

Narrowing my choice to one sentence was difficult, and this one has a semi-colon, so I'm fudging a bit, but it's the passage that first came to mind and the one I kept coming back to. I use this to open up conversation when I teach *A Farewell to Arms* because it illustrates how Hemingway lays the groundwork for the rest of the book. If we're looking beneath his iceberg here, we might not be as surprised by the direction the novel will take.

We remember this scene when we read the Caporetto section and the childbirth scene at the end. Are you suggesting that many of the major movements in the novel are collapsed into this early sentence?

Exactly. Once you know the novel, once you've read all the way to the end and come back and look at this sentence, you see that the kernel of the book is there, that it foreshadows everything. I was reminded of *Silver Linings Playbook* and a memorable scene with Bradley Cooper's character in the film. He has stayed up until 4:00 a.m. reading *A Farewell to Arms*, and when he finishes, he curses, throws the book out the window, and bursts into his parents' bedroom to vent his frustration. He has expected this nice happy ending because the two young lovers, Catherine and Frederic, go off together and they're going to have a baby, but the baby dies and then Catherine dies. Cooper's character is so furious. He obviously didn't see the foreshadowing that this sentence brings.

You mentioned the semicolon. This is a long, complex sentence. When people think of writing that's Hemingwayesque, they might think of tough, terse prose, simple declarative sentences; however, what I'm getting here is that the content might be Hemingwayesque but the style may not normally be associated with his writing. Is that fair to say?

Yes, your assessment is absolutely fair. When I think of Hemingway's writing, when we all do, what comes to mind is concise, reportorial sentences. Just the facts laid down for us by listing what the soldiers are carrying, what conditions they experience as they march forward. But then he inserts this odd phrase "gone with child" to describe how they look. We know Catherine will literally die giving birth. So, in this complicated passage, what I see as the essence of truth, Hemingway has put it all in using his stylistic shorthand.

—

"Rather than 'one true sentence,'
I might use the phrase 'one true emotion'..."

—

To give you an example of the problem in choosing only one or the other side of the semicolon, let me offer a similar construction coming at the end of the opening chapter: "At the start of the winter came the permanent rain and with the rain came the cholera." There's a simple declarative sentence, but what's missing is what's really important, the impactful second phrase: "But it was checked and in the end only seven thousand died of it in the army." You can't read the second sentence because "it" isn't defined. We don't know what the "it" is. It's cholera. But you can't read the first sentence without the second sentence to know the power of the word "only." I found that to be true about most of Hemingway's short, declarative sentences. You need either the sentence before it or the sentence after it to impact the power of that concise sentence.

When you said "six months gone with child," I realized that's such a surprise ending. There's almost a mini-narrative right there at the end.

Who would ever pair soldiers marching with a pregnant woman? It's just an odd pairing and more powerful because of the oddness of it.

Does Hemingway ever use that phrase anywhere else?

Not that I know. "Gone with child" is an unusual phrase. I looked it up, and it seems to be a British idiom. We know *In Our Time* has some words and phrases that have a British tone, and this still seeps into his writing in *A Farewell to Arms*. I find it particularly effective here. I mean, the power of just that word "gone" is wonderful.

Do you think there is something about studying Hemingway that lends itself to a "one true sentence" approach, whereas that approach wouldn't be as fruitful with another writer like Edith Wharton or F. Scott Fitzgerald? Or do you think you might be able to study any writer in such an atomistic way?

I think about why Hemingway is so popular, not just in the U.S. but also internationally. He translates well because the sentences are easy to read, but this doesn't diminish how complex they are too. Maybe he's not unique, though in significant ways I believe he is, but Hemingway is certainly one that so many writers that came after him talk about as being the model.

Rather than "one true sentence," I might use the phrase "one true emotion," where a sentence becomes a sort of objective correlative for the feeling he wants the reader to absorb. The one true emotion in *A Farewell to Arms* is doom, the sense of humanity being doomed with this war.

When you say "true emotion" or "true sentence," what do you think Hemingway means by "true"?

I don't believe he means factually true but rather that it feels authentic. I think Hemingway is looking for what is true to the human condition, that this story resonates with anyone. You don't have to be a soldier. You don't have to know someone who dies in childbirth to feel the poignancy of what he's sharing.

➤·◄

GAIL SINCLAIR is an independent scholar whose publications include co-editing *War + Ink: New Perspectives on Ernest Hemingway's Early Life and Writings* and *Key West Hemingway: A Reassessment*, as well as essays in *Hemingway's Women: Female Critics and the Female Voice, Teaching Hemingway's* A Farewell to Arms, *Approaches to Teaching Fitzgerald's* The Great Gatsby, *Ernest Hemingway in Context, Edith Wharton in Context,* and *F. Scott Fitzgerald in Context.*

JAMES PLATH

ONE TRUE SENTENCE FROM
"Big Two-Hearted River"

What is your one true sentence and why?

I really like one that's descriptively vivid, artful, and suggestive of a deeper meaning: "As the shadow of the kingfisher moved up the stream, a big trout shot upstream in a long angle, only his shadow marking the angle, then lost his shadow as he came through the surface of the water, caught the sun, and then, as he went back into the stream under the surface, his shadow seemed to float down the stream with the current, unresisting, to his post under the bridge where he tightened facing up into the current."

It's true that Hemingway frequently used simple declarative sentences—something he attributed to his time working at the *Kansas City Star*—but he did not use such sentences exclusively. In that well-known passage from *A Moveable Feast*, when Hemingway stalled, he reminded himself, "All you have to do is write one true sentence. Write the truest sentence that you know." And what young Hemingway knew best and missed most, according to a letter he wrote his parents from a hospital bed in Milan, was fishing in northern Michigan. Though he wrote about his summers "up north" in previous stories, "Big Two-Hearted River" was his first fishing story, and you can almost picture him trying to recall the exact sensations he experienced when he fished those waters. Paul Smith tells us that Hemingway was working on "Big Two-Hearted River" on March 20, 1925, when he wrote his father, "I'm trying in all my stories to get the feeling of the actual life across—not to just depict life—or criticize it—but to actually make it alive. So that when you have read something by me you actually experience the thing." In the kingfisher sentence, I think Hemingway succeeds in doing that, and in a poetic manner. He also manages to suggest a symbolic or metaphoric level by his repetition of the word "shadow" four times in this single sentence, as if to suggest the persistent shadow of the war that has accompanied Nick home.

Jim, you're known for your book, *The 100 Greatest Literary Characters*. Is Nick Adams one of the greatest?

You know, he would have made the 200s. This was a tough one. I mean, who do you get? Do you get Jake Barnes or do you get Brett Ashley? Do you get Robert Jordan or do you go with Santiago? Since one of our main points for organizing this was to get characters that had burst the confines of their pages, we went with Santiago because he's made more of a ripple effect beyond literature, with *The Old Man and the Sea* and all of the archetypal associations there.

Top 200—we'll settle for that! Who is Nick Adams? Who is he to Hemingway? And why is he a great literary character?

To me, Nick Adams *is* Ernest Hemingway, thinly disguised. He's about the same age. He has about the same experiences. He has about the same loves and fears, likes and dislikes. When we encounter him in "Big Two-Hearted River," he's a devoted fisherman, as was Ernest. It's important to note that before Ernest went to war, before he went to serve in the Red Cross ambulance corps, the last thing he did, on April 30, 1918, was go with a fellow *Kansas City Star* writer, Ted Brumback, and they met up with Carl Edgar and Charlie Hopkins, and they went on a fishing trip. Then, when he got back from the war, after he recovered, after he went to Oak Park and spent a little time with his family until he couldn't stand it anymore, the very next thing he did was—yep, you guessed it!—go right back to Michigan's Upper Peninsula on a fishing trip, on May 30, 1919. He went this time with Bill Horne, Bill Smith, and Hopkins again. So, fishing trips up north bookended Hemingway's wartime experience.

In your description of the background or inspiration for "Big Two-Hearted River," you mentioned that Hemingway went as part of a group of friends, twice; however, in the story Nick is all by himself. Why that shift?

If you go with a group of friends, then it's just another buddy journey. If you go alone, then now suddenly you have a more interiorized account instead of a group of guys drinking beer and catching fish. It shifts the focus to Nick himself.

—

"Maybe it was deliberately deemphasized, the whole idea of plot, narrative, anything happening, so that he could focus on description, he could focus on one true sentence about one true country."

—

Here's something that I was thinking about just earlier this morning: when this story was first published in 1925, in *This Quarter* magazine, then again as part of that second *In Our Time* collection, that was just seven years after World War I had ended. Given Nick's age and the fact that he's able to hike like a foot soldier with a heavily loaded backpack for miles and miles and set up camp by himself, I think that readers likely would have assumed that

Nick was a returning war veteran. Whereas now my students read the story and that's the furthest thing from their minds. There are no clues about the war in the story. So, I think by having Nick be alone, it kind of plays out on so many different fronts, to use that war metaphor. It sets the stage for themes of loss and introspection, where you just wouldn't have gotten that if he'd been accompanied by other fishing mates.

Fitzgerald said that Hemingway had written a story where nothing happens. When you look at the plot of "Big Two-Hearted River," with all the walking, making camp, and fishing, it doesn't seem to have the eventfulness of a typical short story. Is that fair to say?

It is, and Hemingway even admitted in a letter that it was really a story where nothing happens, but the *country*. For him, it was getting the country right. Getting the country right was enough for Cézanne, and it was enough for Hemingway, who wrote of Nick in a deleted section from "Big Two-Hearted River," "He wanted to write like Cezanne [sic] painted." That mattered in this story; the narrative itself was unimportant. Maybe it was deliberately deemphasized, the whole idea of plot, narrative, anything happening, so that he could focus on description, he could focus on one true sentence about one true country.

Is this precisely part of the point about Nick's character? He's been traumatized by World War I and is looking to recuperate in nature?

Nature, of course, has this reputation among poets as being restorative. You mentioned this consensus interpretation, which is that the story is about war. As I said, there's really no mention of the war. Yet, that's the consensus reading based on what Hemingway wrote in *A Moveable Feast*, which was published posthumously, where he said, "The story was about coming back from the war but there was no mention of the war in it."

Now, here's my question for you: when a writer doesn't include anything, not even the slightest hint in a story that something is about something, then says it outside of the story, how do we treat that?

You're asking a very fair question, but can we really say there's absolutely no hint of the war in this story?

I mean, there are some instances, sure, like where he says, "Now things were done. There had been this to do. Now it was done. It had been a hard trip. He was very tired. That was done. He had made his camp. He was settled. Nothing could touch him." Just the fact of adding that last "Nothing could touch him" indicates a level of, I don't know if you'd call it fear or paranoia, or even a gentle foreboding. It indicates that maybe there's something in his backstory, whether it's war, whether it's something else that's traumatic, that there's something there.

➤•◄

JAMES PLATH is R. Forrest Colwell Endowed Chair & Professor of English at Illinois Wesleyan University. He is a film critic and a prolific scholar of modern American literature, focusing on F. Scott Fitzgerald, John Updike, and Ernest Hemingway. One of his recent books (along with co-authors Gail Sinclair and Kirk Curnutt) is *The 100 Greatest Literary Characters*.

ANDRE DUBUS III

ONE TRUE SENTENCE FROM

"Hills Like White Elephants"

What is your one true sentence and why?

Well, I could give you five hundred of them for Hemingway, but my choice is the opening line of his masterful short story, "Hills Like White Elephants": "The hills across the valley of the Ebro were long and white." But I have to read you the next line because that first line, the reason I love it so much, necessarily created the second: "On this side there was no shade and no trees and the station was between two lines of rails in the sun." Third line: "Close against the side of the station there was the warm shadow of the building and a curtain, made of strings of bamboo beads, hung across the open door into the bar, to keep out flies."

We all know that the heart of character-driven fiction is of course *character*. I would argue that the lungs therefore are *place*. And if you don't ground your characters in a real three-dimensional space, a landscape (urban, rural, interior, exterior, what have you), your characters will literally not be able to breathe and they will stop functioning as real people.

So, there are many reasons why I think that opening line is the perfect, true sentence, but one of those other reasons is that, with "On this side there was no shade," Hemingway is now coming around to who is in this place. And to read one more line, "The American and the girl with him sat at a table in the shade, outside the building. It was very hot and the express from Barcelona would come in forty minutes. It stopped at this junction for two minutes and went on to Madrid." Now on one level you could think, well, there's nothing very interesting about all that. It's very informational, almost journalistic. And, of course, Hemingway was a reporter in his early years. But it does more than that.

I would say it's profluent. It all leans towards the opening line of dialogue. "'What should we drink?' the girl asked. She had taken off her hat and put it on the table. 'It's pretty hot,' the man said." As someone who's been trying to cultivate, for a few decades of my adult life, that Flannery O'Connor idea that "there's a certain grain of stupidity that the writer of fiction can hardly do without, and this is the quality of having to stare," I would argue that it is absolutely essential that we learn to simply wait for the true thing and then reach for the words that make that thousand-mile journey from the interior of the writer to the page and ultimately into the reader. As you know, Hemingway was a pioneer and a master of that. And I'm very grateful to him for it.

In the sequence that you read, we go from the panorama and a consideration of Spain to the string of bamboo. So, when you're talking about place, are you talking about the atmosphere in which the characters are, or the tangible physical room or the chair that they're on, that kind of concrete actuality?

All of the above. John Gardner coined the phrase "psychic distance," which means the distance the reader feels from the events of the story. Hemingway begins in a very cinematic way. The camera's actually panning from far right: "The hills across the valley of the Ebro were long and white." And then we come to the train station and now we're at the table and now we're at the girl and the man, and they're wondering what they're going to drink.

So, it's a wonderful winnowing down of being far away. And then moving in closer and closer and closer. And now we are invested in knowing who these people are, where they're going, what they're going to drink. Nothing happens in this story except for what they talk about. And the fact that the man is trying to get the woman to do something she doesn't want to do. And it's all through dialogue.

One of the main reasons I teach this story a lot is that it was published in 1927. It's almost a hundred years old, but I never let my students know how old this story is. They're always shocked because it seems so modern to them. It seems so contemporary to them, even though the language is different and they're clearly people from a different time. But I find that remarkable and beautiful.

Are your students waiting for action?

Yeah. Sadly. They are waiting for action, but I'm always moved and beyond pleased, when it's very rare that a student of mine doesn't love this story and isn't grateful even if very little happened. They're smart, they're sensitive, they're alive. They know what's going on. And so many of them, especially with the male-female relations, identify the dominant man and the submissive woman, who's running this relationship and who's going to get hurt.

How do you read that last line, when the woman says, "There's nothing wrong with me. I feel fine"? How does this story end for you?

Oh, they're screwed. I mean, stepping out at the rail station, having a beer, having an anise before they get back on the train, she may very well get the procedure he wants her to get. And I don't want to say it out loud in case someone hasn't read this story yet. But she knows that they are through.

—

"He was trying to give the experience, not depict it, but to give the reader the experience ..."

—

There's so much gray in this story, and I'm still not convinced that she's going to leave him. I'm still not convinced that she's going to stop loving him. I am convinced that she's feeling deeply at this moment, something very clear, which is that he does not love her and maybe never has. And it's all between the lines and the great master has trusted us to get it, because we're people, too.

One of the intersections between your work and Hemingway's, I would say, is the aptly chosen detail. I'm interested in that aptitude that you have for choosing a collection of details or that one detail that will render a lived experience. Is that something that you're conscious of?

Can I read another Hemingway line? This is from *Death in the Afternoon*: "For myself ... the problem was one of depiction and waking in the night I tried to remember what it was that seemed just out of my remembering and that was the thing that I had really seen and, finally, remembering all around it, I got it. When he [the matador] stood up, his face white and dirty and the silk of his breeches opened from waist to knee, it was the dirtiness of the rented breeches, the dirtiness of his slit underwear and the clean, clean, unbearably clean whiteness of the thigh bone that I had seen, and it was that which was important."

I love that so much! And when I first read that as a young writer in my twenties, I was so inspired. I couldn't sleep for days because I realized, he was trying to give the experience, not depict it, but to give the reader the experience of being in, say a bullring, watching a matador gored, to give it fully to the reader. And to me, that's such a generous act, which took immense discipline. Thank God he was able to pull it off many, many times in his life.

>-<

ANDRE DUBUS III's seven books include the *New York Times* bestsellers *House of Sand and Fog, The Garden of Last Days,* and his memoir, *Townie.* He has been a finalist for the National Book Award and has been awarded a Guggenheim Fellowship, the National Magazine Award for Fiction, two Pushcart Prizes, and is a recipient of an American Academy of Arts and Letters Award in Literature.

JENNIFER HAIGH

"Mr. and Mrs. Elliot"

What is your one true sentence and why?

My sentence is from the story "Mr. and Mrs. Elliot" that was published in Hemingway's first collection *In Our Time*. The sentence is, "They tried as often as Mrs. Elliot could stand it." It's the second sentence of the story. For context, I'm going to give you the paragraph: "Mr. and Mrs. Elliot tried very hard to have a baby. They tried as often as Mrs. Elliot could stand it. They tried in Boston after they were married and they tried coming over on the boat. They did not try very often on the boat because Mrs. Elliot was quite sick. She was sick and when she was sick she was sick as Southern women are sick. That is women from the Southern part of the United States. Like all Southern women Mrs. Elliot disintegrated very quickly under sea sickness, travelling at night, and getting up too early in the morning. Many of the people on the boat took her for Elliot's mother. Other people who knew they were married believed she was going to have a baby. In reality she was forty years old. Her years had been precipitated suddenly when she started travelling."

So, this one true sentence comes very early in this story that is really a forensic examination of a young, ill-advised marriage between this very unlikely young husband and significantly older wife. What I find remarkable about the sentence, and about the story in general, is Hemingway's use of point of view. It's this kind of distant voice that tells you the facts of the story as the people involved understand them and as they relay them to each other. This narrative voice does not question the veracity of any of the official version of this marriage. The voice simply reports, "This is how this marriage has unfolded." As the story progresses, you come to see that there are fundamental fissures in this marriage that neither the husband nor the wife talks about or perhaps can articulate, but what we are given is the official version of events, how things happen and the official explanation.

It calls to mind Hemingway's reputation for objectivity in narration. As you read the story, you're wondering how objective is this narrator really? Does he tip his hand? Is he tongue-in-cheek?

The narrative voice is very knowing. You sense that it knows much more than it is telling you. It simply states the official version of events without analysis, without judgment, without theorizing or speculating as to the truth of any of the facts. Of course, as modern readers we draw other conclusions about the motivations of Mr. and Mrs. Elliot, as Hemingway means for us to do.

With Hemingway, it's always a balance between what is revealed and what is omitted—his iceberg principle of writing. As a Hemingway reader, how do you respond to his theory of omission? How do you enact it as a writer and negotiate that balance?

Hemingway gives the reader a lot of credit. There's never an attempt to interpret the characters' motivations for us. He trusts us to figure it out on our own. Especially in these early stories, there's very little internality, as such. We aren't inside these people's heads; we're simply hearing the story as they would tell it.

—

"I didn't know how to write a sentence until I read Hemingway."

—

As a writer, I've gone through several cycles of this. Early on, when I was highly influenced by Hemingway, there was very little internality in my own early stories as well, and it was for me as a young writer a really important lesson. I didn't know how to write a sentence until I read Hemingway. And I do think if you look at twentieth-century American literature, he had a cauterizing effect on the way fiction writers wrote sentences. If you look at what predates Hemingway—a writer like Henry James or, later, Thomas Wolfe—there is a fulsome quality to those sentences that Hemingway cut right through. He had a remarkable clarifying effect on language generally. We all write differently because Hemingway wrote the way he wrote.

The first sentence of the story is "Mr. and Mrs. Elliot tried very hard to have a baby." Although that's a very simple-sounding sentence, I'm not sure how frequently it's described that way, that you've "tried very hard to have a baby." Are the characters being mocked or pitied by the narrator, or is he just presenting their activity?

He's presenting their activity as they would themselves render it. There is a real stealth humor in this story, completely subterranean. There's nothing overt about it. He's never disrespectful toward the characters, but there is implicit comedy in some of their difficulties. You sense that the narrative voice is very much aware of this. You also see it when he talks about other people's reactions to this odd marriage. I love this sentence: "His mother cried when he brought Cornelia home after their marriage but brightened very much when she learned they were going to live abroad." There's no explanation of why the mother cried or why she might have been relieved that they were going to move far away. It's simply stated that this was her position.

And then at the end of the story, "They had many a good cry together," which means something altogether different, right?

The story ends very wonderfully with an uncharacteristically complex sentence for the young Hemingway. The final sentence is, "In the evening they all sat at dinner together in the garden under a plane tree and the hot evening wind blew and Elliot drank white wine and Mrs. Elliot and the girl friend made conversation and they were all quite happy."

Thinking about your writing career, are there times where it really is one true sentence that galvanizes an entire project?

Yes. It's particularly true in a first draft, which I really do write sentence-by-sentence. My friend Andre Dubus says that the next sentence always lies in the last sentence you wrote. And it's really just following a chain. I truly believe in Hemingway's mantra: if you write a true sentence, then you go on from there; that one true sentence will lead to another true sentence.

Doesn't that make the first sentence of the novel of the utmost importance?

It does, and yet you almost never get it on the first go. That's the difficulty of writing a first draft: knowing that much of what you're writing is wrong and that a lot of it is going to have to be thrown away. It's hard to proceed with that knowledge, but you must keep going in order to get to the good stuff. Sometimes you have to write through some sentences that are not true. This is the danger of Hemingway's dictum. If you take it too much to heart, you can endlessly question the truth of the sentence you've just written and never get to sentence two.

Let's talk about truth. How can a sentence be true?

I think it's really a question of exactitude. It's not qualifying to make things gentler. It's not modifying endlessly to convey these kinds of modulations of tone. As a young writer I tended to soften things. When I'm teaching, I often see this tendency in young female students. I think it has to do with the fact that girls are raised to please. I was trained from birth to put things delicately and diplomatically, and that can get in the way of writing a true sentence. You try so hard to convey these small gradations of meaning, so as not to make the truth too upsetting or objectionable to anybody, and really you can modify yourself right out of ever writing anything true.

What's the relationship, if any, between that kind of modification that you're talking about and the iceberg principle, where you can convey something without actually coming right out and saying it?

It's a question of modifiers and verbs. Young writers tend to rely excessively on adverbs, not understanding that if you feel a need to put an adverb in a sentence, it probably means that the verb is lacking. I see this sometimes with students. They construct these fabulously elaborate adverbial clauses and it's really just because they haven't found the right verb. The bones of the sentence are not strong enough.

Then you read something like *The Great Gatsby*, where Fitzgerald writes "'Can't repeat the past?' he cried incredulously." Are you going to circle "incredulously" and say that's too much? Or are you going to say, "Congratulations on writing one of the most famous lines in the great American novel"?

It's hard for me to quibble with anything in *Gatsby*, I will tell you. And any sort of pronouncement I can make about writing, that novel probably violates.

I read it probably once a year. It's so very dear to my heart, and I so admire it. And yet I don't understand how you do that.

Hemingway uses these very simple dialogue tags because he trusts the truth of the dialogue he has written. Often what I'll see in my own bad first drafts or another writer's bad first draft is that you write a completely inadequate line of dialogue, and then you feel the need to apply a lot of stage directions. So, if you say this just the right way, it will seem meaningful. If the dialogue is good enough, it needs no further explanation, like that terrific line you quoted. It doesn't matter how he said it.

If you're a writer who is writing in that style, are you at peace knowing that readers will have a range of interpretations, that they'll hear it a number of different ways within a given scope?

I don't think they will, if you get the dialogue right. When you nail it, the dialogue is so revelatory, so meaningful, that there's no other way it can be taken.

➤·◄

JENNIFER HAIGH is the PEN/Hemingway Award-winner for *Mrs. Kimble.* She went on to publish five more books of fiction— most recently, *Heat and Light,* which won a Literature Award from the American Academy of Arts and Letters and was named a Best Book of 2016 by the *New York Times.*

ADRIAN SPARKS

What is your one true sentence and why?

In his introduction to *Treasury for the Free World*, Hemingway wrote, "Never think that war, no matter how necessary, nor how justified, is not a crime." In today's environment of "spin," half-truths, and outright lies, a sentence like this is a beacon. I grew up in the 1950s watching the glamorized world of war on TV. My father, who before becoming a minister served in the British Navy, would comment often on the danger of such a glib presentation of an awful reality. Later, in the 1960s, I marched against the Vietnam conflict and although I was lucky enough to have not been drafted, I had close friends whose lives were irrevocably shattered by their experience. Hemingway was there, in the midst of war, and he too was marked by the experience.

The simple eloquence of that sentence. Brilliant.

You mention watching portrayals of war in the 1950s. Was Hemingway part of your education and your coming of age as an artist?

It actually began in puberty. Hemingway was one of the first people to write about what it feels like for a man to be in love. Prior to that, it was generally what it feels like for a woman to be in love, and the man was just an action figure. So, he actually guided me through puberty. *The Sun Also Rises* was very profound for me.

—

"Hemingway was one of the first people to write about what it feels like for a man to be in love."

—

So, it began at an early age and then fast-forward forty-plus years and an actress backstage at a show I was doing in Los Angeles knocked on my door and said, "You know, my folks just saw this play on Broadway. You would just be perfect for it." And it was Len Cariou doing the play *Papa* on Broadway.

Following that I got in touch with the playwright John DeGroot. He has a Pulitzer Prize for his coverage of the Kent State shootings. And he too is a Hemingway fan. So, he did a huge amount of research, and this one-man show is an hour and a half of Hemingway talking non-stop. The conceit of the play is that Hemingway's just found out Mary has left and they've had a huge fight and the audience members are journalists from *Life* magazine who've come to interview him and showed up unannounced. You go on a journey with him.

Your portrayal in that play of course led to the film *Papa: Hemingway in Cuba*. That film was the first production in Cuba—

Since 1958.

How did the Cubans respond to your presence?

It was revelatory for me. It gave me such an understanding of him. During my time on that island, so many strangers approached me with big smiles, because they just wanted to talk to Papa. I'd go to the beach for the afternoon and you'd just hear "Papa! Papa!" Every old Cuban had a Hemingway interaction story. Gladys Rodriguez Ferrero was the head of the Hemingway estate there, and she took me around on a day off to all the old Hemingway haunts. She just knew everything, delightful ninety-year-old Cuban woman. We get to Cienfuegos, a port on the southern coast of Cuba, where Hemingway docked his boat. And I'm wearing the hairpiece, I'm wearing the whole Hemingway outfit because it's being done for a "behind the scenes" filming. So, I'm looking like Hemingway. I'm standing on a dock and I hear this scream coming from the land and this old woman is waving, screaming. We went up to her, and Gladys is translating this old woman who is saying, "When I was a little girl, I was standing by my gate and you came along and you told me, 'Don't cry,' because I'm a beautiful princess." Oh my God. We actually shot that scene but it didn't make it into the final cut. He's absolutely adored there.

That has to be the type of experience that enhances the performance.

It's priceless.

Interestingly enough, it's all women that run the Hemingway estate. You go there and you feel as if you've entered a monastery, a convent. There's such an adoration, such a holiness to this place. And there was a real attitude right when I first arrived, I could see there was a real circumspect looking at me— *who's this guy that's going to be playing our savior?*—kind of thing. I could feel it. It was palpable. They never left the set. There was a woman posted at every doorway. If somebody happened to touch a bookcase, they were right there. So, they're watching the whole process right from the beginning.

We're doing the scene when Hemingway is struggling with writer's block. I am standing on this exact square foot of ground that Hemingway stood on when he wrote at the exact same bookcase. We had brought a replacement prop for everything, including his typewriter, and we were about to start filming. And I looked down the hallway and it's like a procession: three women with one woman in the lead carrying what I later learned was Hemingway's typewriter. And they said, "We'd like Adrian to use this." Knock me over with a feather. So, that typewriter you see in the film, that's his typewriter. That's not a prop. When I'm touching that typewriter, I'm touching the master's typewriter.

Incredible. Adrian, your depiction of Hemingway is certainly the opposite of his blustering Papa stereotype.

He was not the macho guy. He was actually a very, very sensitive man. He was one of the first writers to understand the power of a public image, which he definitely exploited—mastered, actually. The film is a true story. It's written by a journalist named Denne Bart Petitclerc, it's his story of how he wound up spending several years with the Hemingway family until they left Cuba for the States when things got pretty dicey there. This is a tough time in Hemingway's life. He's actually dying and doesn't know that. He had had plane crashes, and it was a very slow death, but that's what killed him. His body was shutting down. So, it was an emotional time, deeply emotional. He'd lost the ability to write. He couldn't make love anymore. You know, what is there left to live for? Ultimately, of course, he decided that there wasn't anything worth living for.

The Hemingway you portrayed in your movie was a very complex figure. Within a single scene, Hemingway could show bravado and could be pathetic. He could be so sensitive. And wrathful. He could be angry and temperamental and boisterous and fun all in the matter of a scene.

That's lovely feedback. That's what we did. That's what we were going for. He was bipolar. He was diabetic. He was an alcoholic. That's a perfect storm right there. It was before they understood what it was and how to treat that. He finally received shock treatment at the Mayo Clinic.

Hotchner was one of my big go-tos for understanding who this man was. He tells a great story. Excuse me, sometimes I get emotional telling this story because it's very connected to who this guy was. But, he's at the Mayo Clinic. He's gone through all these shock treatments. And Hotchner writes in his book, there Hemingway was, he was the guy I knew. He was full of life. He was happy. There was joy. It was just wonderful to see him. Apparently, Hemingway said, "Come on, Hotch, let's go outside." And they went outside. The second he got outside, he said, "I know what those fuckers are doing." The cheerfulness was a performance. And shortly after that, he was released, and he tried to run into the propeller of an airplane that was taking him back to Ketchum. And we know what happened then.

→•←

ADRIAN SPARKS is a film and stage actor with an almost endless list of credits, from classical theatre like Shakespeare, to *The West Wing* and *Ally McBeal*. Born in the United Kingdom, he received an Ovation Award in 2005 for his portrayal of Ernest Hemingway in the one-man play, *Papa*, by John DeGroot. He also portrayed Hemingway in the film *Papa: Hemingway in Cuba*.

PAUL HENDRICKSON

ONE TRUE SENTENCE FROM
A Moveable Feast

What is your one true sentence and why?

There are so many one true sentences. Mine would have to do with water, Hemingway and water, and his boat *Pilar*. So, the sentence is in a little section of *A Moveable Feast* called "The People of the Seine": "I could never be lonely along the river." He's talking about going down to the river and watching the old Parisian fishermen with their "long, jointed, cane poles" bringing home "a few *fritures*," which is a very tasty, salty fish.

He didn't ever fish in the Seine. He took his tackle to Spain, but he would just get infinite pleasure by taking a big wad of bread and some sausage and going down the stone quays off the Pont Neuf. In a sense, Hemingway gave up rivers for the ocean, for the Gulf Stream. The fluidity of moving water is one of the great truisms of his life.

When you think of Hemingway's association with rivers or with bodies of water, *A Moveable Feast* and Paris aren't really what first comes to mind.

As a child, it was one linear mile from his porch step on Kenilworth Avenue in Oak Park to the not especially beautiful Des Plaines River. The seventeenth-century explorers Marquette and Joliet paddled the Des Plaines, which eventually, if you follow it far enough, will lead you to the Mississippi, and the Mississippi will lead you into the Gulf of Mexico. So, one linear mile from Hemingway's front porch was an ungainly river where he could catch fish, and there are beautiful pictures of him as a child leaning against the river-bank of the Des Plaines. From earliest memory on—let alone those gorgeous trout streams in northern Michigan—that's what we would associate Hemingway and rivers with.

In your book and oftentimes in Hemingway's own letters, his boat appears as a character. So, *Pilar* is a woman. What was her personality?

Wonderful question. Yeah, I think *Pilar* was his greatest lover. *Pilar* outlasted four wives, all his ruin, the Nobel Prize, etc. *Pilar* was faithful. *Pilar* was constant. *Pilar* was always purring down there at the dock. Even when the engines weren't turned on, twelve miles from his house at the Finca Vigía outside Havana, she was waiting in the harbor for him. She was faithful and those engines would turn over. They very rarely disappointed him. Yes, every once in a while something went wrong and they had to have an overhaul, but this lover, mistress, wife named *Pilar*—and this tender feminine presence was named *Pilar* because he always said that, if he had a daughter, he would have named her *Pilar*—so *Pilar*, his lover, his wife, his daughter is just there for him. And she performs too, by the way. She ain't no doormat.

Your book also contains the specs and Hemingway's requirements for this boat. Were those out of the ordinary? Did Hemingway know what he was doing?

He did. He studied. The previous nine months, he and his second wife, Pauline Pfeiffer, were away from their family, away from Key West, away from the children. They were on safari. They weren't on safari the entire time, but they were away nine months in Europe and in Africa. His suitcase was stuffed with brochures from boat manufacturers. He was a scholar, he was a student, he was a scientist, which he got from his father. He wasn't going to make a commitment until he knew what he wanted. So, he decided on the Wheeler boat manufacturing company.

—

"The fluidity of moving water is one of the great truisms of his life."

—

And I'm not a boat person, I'm a fisherman. I'm a watery person, but I'm not a boat man. And I'm not an ocean fishermen, but I got somebody expert in the history of these 1930s boats. And they told me to think of *Pilar* as not a sexy Cadillac nor a thrifty Ford, but somewhere in the middle, maybe a Buick. This was not a custom boat as many people think. This was a factory boat that came off the line, but he had it cut to his specifications. By the time he got home from Europe and Africa, and they went out to the Wheeler shipyard, he knew exactly what he wanted. He asked that the transom be cut down low for being able to haul the big fish in more easily from the stern. He wanted a big roller bar to help roll it. And he had other specifications that were built on to this factory boat. And over the years, of course, he modified it. He built the flying bridge up top. That was not there on the original boat.

Pilar is, by these vintage standards of wooden boats in the 1930s, a beautiful looking object, but she was not an exquisitely skinny racing kind of yacht. No, *Pilar* was bulkier than that. *Pilar* was clunkier than that in a way, except she had a lot of speed. We all remember that beautiful description of Lady Brett Ashley in *The Sun Also Rises*: "She was built with curves like the hull of a racing yacht."

One of my favorite things that your book introduces is not only the history of *Pilar*, but also you advance an argument about how his ownership of and experiences with this boat affected his writing career, his writing style. You write: "The art of slacking, of holding back before you try to set the hook, is counterintuitive, counterreflexive, which is probably why Hemingway was so damn good at it—in both fishing and literature."

That's wonderful. I'm a fly fisherman. I'm a trout fishermen, and the art of slacking applies. Your instinct, your instantaneous impulse is to jerk on the rod. But if you do that, you'll jerk the fly right out of the trout's mouth. And if you do that with big game rigs, you will jerk the live bait fish that you have on the hook out of the marlin's mouth. So, you have to *slack* to him. And what does slack to him mean? It means that against every impulse, you have to wait a beat or two or three for the hook to get set, and then you can begin working the fish in. But if you jerk, you're lost.

And I use the word "jerk," which is pregnant. Hemingway could be such a jerk on his boat. I'm using the word in a different sense right there, but there are letters and documents and other evidences where he could go into a fury when one of his guests on his boat, John Dos Passos or somebody, did not slack to him. And then the fish gets lost. So, rather than sort of saying, "Well, let me show you how to do this" (although in another sense, he was a great teacher and he was a great teacher with his sons), his anger could boil over and he could scream, "You didn't *slack* to him!"

So, what is the literary equivalent of slacking? Is it, like you, waiting twenty years from getting the idea for this book, letting it percolate and then finally writing it? Or is it sentence by sentence, letting a story unfold? How did Hemingway slack in his own art?

I think your questions are almost too weighty for me. I think it's all of the above. I think it's both/and. Everybody who studies Hemingway knows about the so-called iceberg theory. In a sense, isn't that a first cousin of slacking? In *Death in the Afternoon,* there's a phrase that he uses, which I so love: "The dignity of movement of an ice-berg." The dignity of an iceberg derives from the fact that seven-eighths are underwater. There is a slacking in the sense that I'm only going to tell you one-eighth of this story and allow your own imagination to loll around the edges of the hook, which is what a big fish does.

The reason you have to slack, even with a trout, is that a trout can hit it like a torpedo, but at the same time, if you jerk it, you're going to miss it. I think of my own slacking in letting these ideas germinate: I wrote a book about Frank Lloyd Wright, which is the most recent book. Well, hell, the slacking in that book. I mean, I was on a bicycle when I was in third grade and rode past my first Frank Lloyd Wright house in Kankakee, Illinois, but it only took six decades for the slacking to take effect and come around and find me.

➤·◄

PAUL HENDRICKSON has published seven books, most recently *Plagued by Fire: The Dreams and Furies of Frank Lloyd Wright.* He is the author of the 2011 *New York Times* best seller and National Book Critics Circle Award finalist *Hemingway's Boat: Everything He Loved in Life, and Lost.* In 2003, he won the National Book Critics Circle Award for *Sons of Mississippi: A Story of Race and Its Legacy.* His 1996 work about Vietnam, *The Living and the Dead: Robert McNamara and Five Lives of a Lost War,* was a finalist for the National Book Award. He is the recipient of writing fellowships from the Guggenheim Foundation, the National Endowment for the Arts, the Lyndhurst Foundation, and the Alicia Patterson Foundation.

A. SCOTT BERG

What is your one true sentence and why?

It's tough to pick one true sentence, and I've really been tossing and turning about this. The one true sentence I've come up with is the Hemingway sentence that lingers most in my mind. It's the last line of *The Sun Also Rises*: "Isn't it pretty to think so." My reasons are many. First of all, it shows its trueness as a sentence in its utter simplicity. It's so understated, and yet it expresses so much complexity. It is true to character. It's a wonderful line of dialogue. But I think above all, in one word—"pretty"—Hemingway captures the ambiguity of Jake Barnes, his condition, and the character of all the people in that novel. He captures in that sentence the aimlessness of the Lost Generation, which is what that book is all about.

You talk about the ambiguity of the sentence. What is the range of interpretations for what he is saying? You're saying the word "pretty" carries a lot of weight. How do we interpret that for everybody? Or is there one specific reading?

I don't think there is one specific reading. In fact, the wonderful Library of America has just published its first volume of Hemingway works, which concludes with *The Sun Also Rises*. There is something quite special in this particular publication, which is that for the first time we see in print the way Hemingway actually intended this one true sentence to be published and recited. In this Library of America edition, it ends with a period. Since 1926, every other time we've seen that sentence, it has appeared with a question mark. This was a decision the Library of America made very carefully, and they did it justly because they found that in Hemingway's earlier versions and in the galleys, it ended with a period, not a question mark; and some ambitious copy editor probably made the change all on his own. Editor Max Perkins, who probably never even noticed this, because he was not very big on spelling and punctuation himself, just let it go through. This is significant because I don't think Jake Barnes was asking a question. I think he was just tossing off the remark. It was casual, almost cynical. There's something rather sad about it, wistful. For me, the Lost Generation gets encapsulated in those six words.

Like you, I've read it with a question mark every single time I've read the novel, but when I read it with a period at the end, to me it sounds like almost something he's saying to himself.

I think that's well observed. I think he is. He is all but muttering, especially because Brett doesn't always listen anyway.

The full last line is, "'Yes,' I said. 'Isn't it pretty to think so.'" Hemingway doesn't say, "'Yes,' I said ..." and then pack in an adverb or two. And the word "said" doesn't tell us very much as it is. It's ambiguous and suggestive. Isn't that a quintessential aspect of what it means to be Hemingwayesque?

Very much so. This was one of the great and new things about Hemingway and his writing. It ties into his iceberg theory, where so much is left to the reader.

Hemingway is an enormously suggestive writer. I like that you stopped on the word "said," because this is a technique that continues in the works of Elmore Leonard, among many other contemporary writers. Leonard often commented that you don't need to use a different verb every time somebody speaks. Rather than "he articulated" or "he propounded," you could just say, "he said." That's it. We got it. Especially for such a simple throwaway line as this. Almost every time Hemingway writes dialogue, it is nothing more than "he said" and "she said." And the use of the word "yes" just before the one true sentence—this too is part of Hemingway's magic. This is the secret sauce, actually—that Hemingway's writing is subject to so much interpretation in each word, in as simple a word as "yes" or as complicated a word as "pretty."

How was Max Perkins a different editor and maybe even a different friend for Fitzgerald and Hemingway? How do you see that kind of juggling act that Perkins performed?

It begins with a professional tenet to which Perkins held, what he used to tell people who came for advice on how to be a good editor. He'd say, "Don't try to make Shakespeare into Mark Twain. And don't try to make Mark Twain into Shakespeare." You respond to an author because of the distinctive voice that that author brought to you. That was Perkins's great gift. He heard the new thing and fought for it and got it into print, starting with Fitzgerald and then with Hemingway and again with Thomas Wolfe. And in so doing, he never tried to impose his own voice on any of them. He never tried to turn any of his authors into something they didn't want to be, intend to be, or were unable to be.

—

"Hemingway's writing is subject to so much
interpretation in each word, in as simple a word as 'yes'
or as complicated a word as 'pretty.'"

—

He always brought out what these writers had in them by figuring out what each of them was trying to do with his or her books. He also applied that tenet as he got involved in his authors' personal lives. Perkins realized that early in a book's development was when many authors needed help the most. Here's young alcoholic Scott Fitzgerald spending more money than he was making. Perkins could see he was going to have to step in all the time, often fashioning ways of scaring up some money, usually by quickly publishing volumes of his short stories, just so that he could justify giving him a little extra cash through advances from Scribner's. When Scribner's couldn't advance any more, Perkins found himself writing personal checks to the author—just because he couldn't stand to see his young friend fail and because he really wanted to see that next book. In one such instance, that work in progress became *Tender Is the Night*. Whoa! That's quite an investment.

How do you think the death of Perkins affected Hemingway's writing?

To be perfectly honest, I'm not sure his death affected it very much, just as I don't know how much Perkins in his lifetime affected Hemingway's writing. There were very few times when Perkins stepped in and said, "I think the sentence should be this way." One really couldn't work any other way with Hemingway, who strictly edited himself. So, I don't think the writing per se changed. But I think if you look at Hemingway's career, you can see that Perkins was a caring and influential manager—warning him of things that would put off booksellers and readers and in creating a nurturing publishing atmosphere for him, one that would allow Hemingway to keep moving from book to book. I mean, Max Perkins dies in 1947, and you've got *Across the River and into the Trees* published three years later, a decade since his prior novel had been published; and then you've got *The Old Man and the Sea* two years after that. And that's all that Hemingway publishes for the rest of his life, which ended in 1961.

You don't think *Across the River and into the Trees* would have been improved by Perkins?

I like to think Perkins's guidance could have improved that book, but I'm not sure it would have, especially at that point in their careers. Had Perkins lived another two years, I could easily see him writing a letter with a few comments about portions of the book that start to wander. It gets a little lost. But Hemingway was very much in need of flattery at that time—always, really. I do think that he would have sought Perkins's opinion more than anybody else's. You have to remember—and this is something I realized as I was writing the book—other than family, the relationship with Perkins was the longest in Hemingway's life. It was the most enduring positive relationship he ever had, lasting longer than any of his four marriages. It really started in 1925, and they remained joined until 1947, when Perkins died. So, it's hard for me to imagine Perkins thinking about crossing Hemingway at that point. And let's not forget Hemingway's own depression. You've got to factor in his mental health, which was going steadily downhill. I don't think Perkins would have risked too much because crossing him could easily have meant getting crossed off.

>•<

A. SCOTT BERG is the author of five bestselling biographies. *Max Perkins: Editor of Genius* received the National Book Award; in writing *Goldwyn: A Biography,* he was awarded a Guggenheim Fellowship; and his 1998 biography *Lindbergh* won the Pulitzer Prize. For twenty years, Berg was a friend and confidant of Katharine Hepburn; and his biographical memoir *Kate Remembered,* published upon her death in 2003, became the #1 *New York Times* bestseller for most of that summer. His biography of Woodrow Wilson was published in 2013; and in 2018, he edited the Library of America's *World War I and America: Told by the Americans Who Lived It.*

MARK THOMPSON

ONE TRUE SENTENCE FROM

Men at War

Let me propose one true sentence to you, Mark Thompson. Hemingway writes in his introduction to *Men at War*: "The last war"—referring to World War I—"during the years 1915, 1916, 1917, was the most colossal, murderous, mismanaged butchery that has ever taken place on earth. Any writer who said otherwise lied." Now is that Hemingway bombast or is he right?

As you read out that very well-known phrase, I felt myself recoil slightly from what you call the "Hemingway bombast." Was he right? Yes, I suppose numerically he must be right, as far as the history of war has been recorded. And looking at the word "mismanaged" and recalling the inability of commanders in the field to conceive and implement tactics, which would enable them to do anything except throw more soldiers at the enemy guns? I suppose that's true, too. And certainly the Italian front, although much less known outside Italy, Austria, Slovenia, and Croatia than the Western front, did reflect the character of the wider war in respect of murderous and mismanaged butchery.

So, Hemingway's words in that excerpt are very well chosen. He uses "butchery." Was there a quality to the warfare on the Italian front that perhaps was different than it was on the Western front?

Well, we're discussing a metaphor here. I would hesitate to say that the way in which troops were led to and committed to operations that were overwhelmingly likely to lead to their deaths in great numbers was worse on the Italian front than at the Somme or at Verdun or Passchendaele. And I don't think it would be too meaningful, in fact, to try to draw such a comparison.

But I would say that the Italian front, at its worst, was fully as bad as the Western front. The nature of the front was different. The geography was different. Italy was the aggressor and was therefore committing its forces to offensives far more than the other side. These forces had to fight uphill, sometimes on very steep gradients, against an enemy who was securely positioned on the heights above. On some sectors of the front, the Italians confronted vertical cliffs and glaciers. The tactical advantage enjoyed by the defense on all fronts in the war was even greater here. The Italian commanders were at a loss most of the time; they didn't know how to achieve the objectives they had set for themselves. Therefore, they repeatedly threw their forces into offensives where there was very, very little chance that the objective could be attained.

There's a recurring character in your book, Gabriele D'Annunzio, for whom I think you save your harshest words. What were his motives? This is also a man who recurs as a sort of foil anytime that Hemingway talks about Italy and the war.

I don't regard D'Annunzio as a profound thinker about anything and certainly not about politics. He did have a considerable political impact, to be sure. His motivations in this respect were partly ideological (he was an extreme nationalist) and partly commercial, for he was a paid propagandist who used his fluent and vivid pen, and indeed his speeches to argue for intervention. And he did this with great vehemence in the weeks before Italy joined the war in the spring of 1915.

I quote some parts of speeches he made at that time in my book and I described some of those remarks as psychotic. People have suggested once or twice in print that this is loose language on my part, but I don't believe it is. Let me quote a few lines, if I may, from one of these speeches, to give a flavor, not only of D'Annunzio's florid style, but of Italian nationalism at its worst. I keep using the term "nationalist" and, of course, all nationalisms might have features in common, but they have their specificities, too. Italian nationalism in late 1914 and early 1915, when interventionists were attempting to sway public opinion in favor of going to war, did include an almost insane belief that the country needed a gigantic bloodbath in order to confirm its status as a first-class power and toughen the national character. So, let me quote the famous poet welcoming the intervention in May 1915: "We are fighting with arms, we are waging our war, the blood is spurting from the veins of Italy! ... All these people, who yesterday thronged in the streets and squares, loudly demanding war, are full of veins, full of blood; and that blood begins to flow ...."

So, a little over the top?

Well, yes. It almost sounds grimly comic to us, I suppose, but it certainly wasn't. At the time D'Annunzio exercised a really poisonous influence in the country; this continued after the war, with his coup in Fiume, but that takes us into the post-war period. Suffice to say that I sympathize with the Slovenian artist, Tone Kralj, who painted the interior of a village church near Trieste, during the Second World War. His painting of the parable of the sower portrays the devil, sowing weeds and bullets, using the features of D'Annunzio.

I'd like to connect this to Hemingway. It's Hemingway legend that he described Caporetto so perfectly that Italians could not believe that he

was not in Italy at the time. As you review *A Farewell to Arms*, is that an impressive depiction of World War I?

The section of the novel referred to as "Caporetto" is the canonical account in English of the rout that followed the German-Habsburg breakthrough on the Isonzo front in October 1917. Hemingway worked hard when he was researching it. We know that, and he caught certain aspects of the battle from the Italian point of view wonderfully well.

I remember praising in my book his use of the word "supernatural," where he writes, "They were bent forward and moved smoothly, almost supernaturally, along." He is describing the Italians' impression of the ease and mastery with which the German forces were rampaging ahead. That word is exactly right. The Germans were such wonderful soldiers in both world wars and their participation in the Battle of Caporetto did make the Italian blood run cold. Hemingway caught that.

—

"I remember praising...[Hemingway's] use of the word 'supernatural,'...describing the Italians' impression of the ease and mastery with which the German forces were rampaging ahead. That word is exactly right."

—

However, he somewhat exaggerated that political dimension on the Italian side. An important part in the story is played by a socialist who kills his officer.

Speaking as a historian I feel that is a misrepresentation of what was happening. Apart from Hemingway needing dramatic events for his narrative, he would really have read that the Italian military had been subverted and its morale had been undermined by socialists and defeatists and enemy agents and so forth. This was said a lot at the time during and after the war, and this supposed analysis was echoed by journalists and historians outside Italy as well. But it was not true. The people who spread this interpretation of the Italian defeat, namely as having occurred because the troops had been worm-eaten by internal opponents of the war, abetted by enemy propaganda, wanted to distract attention from the real internal causes, which centered on the destruction of soldiers' morale by sustained failure and brutality at the command level.

So, I always feel when I read that part of Hemingway's novel, that I understand why it's there for dramatic reasons, and because it reflected what most of the available sources were telling him, but it's misleading about the causes of the Italian disaster at Caporetto.

One thing that I find in common with your description in *The White War* and Hemingway's description in *A Farewell to Arms* is the incredible tension and violence between officers and soldiers of the Italian army. You write that "1917 was the year of decimation." When I'm reading the Caporetto section, everybody is basically frightened of one another, and it's really no surprise that Frederic Henry's best friend Bartolomeo Aymo is killed by Italians. It's that type of chaos. Am I misunderstanding what you're saying about that type of violence from officers?

The attitude of senior officers toward their men was often characterized by distance and arrogance. This attitude was worse by autumn 1917 because so many junior officers, who could protect the men to some extent, had been killed, and their replacements were often poorly trained.

Italian morale was also eroded by the disciplinary regime instituted by General Luigi Cadorna, Italy's commander and chief of the general staff. This regime was savage, for example when Cadorna urged the decimation of units judged to have failed in battle. Hemingway catches this aspect of Italy's war unforgettably in the scene of random executions beside the Tagliamento River.

There were some improvements in the treatment of soldiers and their families after Cadorna was removed, at the end of 1917 and in 1918. The data regarding the number of executions after courts martial and summary executions are incomplete, but the data we have show that Italy was extraordinary in this respect. So that's all true. My reservation—and it's only a historian's caveat—is that I'm not aware of political murders of men against officers taking place during the chaotic conditions of the retreat from Caporetto. This is not to deny that such murders may have occurred.

Nevertheless, as a fiction reader I succumb to the Caporetto chapter every time. It's wonderful writing, I would say the best writing in Hemingway's finest novel.

>·<

MARK THOMPSON is a Reader in Modern European History at the University of East Anglia. He has written two books about the disintegration of Yugoslavia in the 1990s, a biography of the writer Danilo Kiš, and a history of Italy in the First World War. This work of history, called *The White War*, received much acclaim when it was published in Britain and the United States in 2010.

SHERMAN ALEXIE

"The Short Happy Life of Francis Macomber"

What is your one true sentence and why?

It's from "The Short Happy Life of Francis Macomber," my favorite Heming-way story: "We all take a beating every day, you know, one way or another."

Just as a sentence, philosophically, it's true. It rings so clearly to me on a personal level, the way I grew up. When you grow up in a violent place emo-tionally, physically, spiritually, you end up feeling that way. You're always flinching. And I felt like I've spent most of my life flinching. Then, the cavalier way the sentence is spoken, that "you know" in the middle of it, which is so true but also so dismissive, so weary. One gets exhausted just by flinching.

In the context of the story, it comes right after Wilson, the hunter, talks about how he beats the natives, the African workers instead of fining them because of the money. So, he beats them to punish them. The sentence imme-diately follows that; it's justification for his behavior. He's so cavalier about the people who work for him, that it reveals something about his brand of mas-culinity, his arrogance, his flouting of the rules and the laws, his mercenary status. It's amazing: he's a hunter, he's this powerful, physical hunter, killer, white man, but he ends up being the fragile one.

The sentence really points out that it's not fatalism per se. It's more like he's given up on any hope in the world. This is just what it is. And this is what is interesting.

Out of context one wouldn't be sure whether this sentence is reassuring or fatalistic. If you say, "Well, we all take a beating," that might be something that could actually give somebody some sort of sustenance, but it could also be something that is immensely discouraging.

Yeah. And it's a shrug because, in the story, Wilson sleeps with Macomber's wife, Margot. She leaves the tent in the middle of the night to go sleep with Wilson and Macomber knows this. I mean, talk about getting a beating. There's all sorts of beatings in the story. And perhaps the worst one is the cruel adultery. I mean, adultery is always cruel, but the particular nature of this incident is breathtaking and for Wilson to treat it as such. It's something that Wilson always does. One of the details that really cuts is that he carries a double cot. You know, I hadn't read this story in a while and when I first read it back as an undergraduate, I did not camp. I was not a camper. So, now after years of having a Boy Scout son you read that story and you're like, "double cot? Oh my God." You get to be this powerful hunter and then you get to have sex with the women who come on the hunt. It made me think, "How many other wives has Wilson slept with?"

———

"The sentence really points out that it's not fatalism per se. It's more like he's given up on any hope in the world. This is just what it is. And this is what is interesting."

———

You've talked about something similar in your poem "Survivorman"—
it actually reads like a corollary of the one true sentence that you just
chose: "Some people want to live more / Than others do. Some can withstand any horror / While others will easily surrender / To thirst, hunger, and extremes of weather." Were you contemplating kind of the same
philosophy?

Wow. I haven't thought about that poem in a long time. I published it a decade
ago or more, and it really does ring true. I got that from that TV series called
Survivorman, and it's a genre of reality television, true stories about people
who have survived extreme circumstances. That poem is based on my memory of an episode where one man carried his friend through the Utah desert to
safety, a marathon of carrying a man on his back and how much he wanted to
live. But more than that, how much more he wanted to save his friend. Could
I have done that walk? I don't think so. I watch these shows and sometimes I
think I could have survived that and sometimes I think, no, I couldn't have,
and I'm sure there's a kind of person who thinks they can survive anything,
who's never been tested and they think they can.

**Are you kind of winking at the reader or are you giving a more serious con-
templation about human capacity?**

I think I'm mocking the reader, our arrogance as human beings, but that
means I'm mocking myself as well. Human capacities are different. I know
there's a lot of talk now about the meritocracy and how some people have
advantages others don't, and that's all true. But still, at the very heart of us,
there are people who want to live more. There are people who will do more
to survive, good or bad. There are people who are just more able to withstand
external circumstances. And I think maybe that's the ultimate measure, right?
I mean, there's always that question of who would you want beside you during
the apocalypse? I always make the joke that, well, you wouldn't want me. I'm

a writer. I have no real-life skills. I type fast. All I can hope is that what works out for me, being a performer and being a comedian, is that maybe I'm entertaining enough to earn a couple salmon, now and again, around the campfire.

When we were talking about Hemingway's one true sentence, does that approach to composition have any overlap to your own writing process?

Oh, that's a great question. Of course, you can write a great prose sentence. And there are many, many examples. I mean, endless. But in poetry, there's the one line, and in most poems you're talking one page. You're talking less than thirty lines. So, the weight of each line matters more. The importance of one line in a poem can determine the course of the entire poem itself. Where with a novel or even a short story, each sentence has less weight, especially in a novel. You can read a great novel, an incredible novel and find bad sentences, even in the best of writers. I can't think of anything off the top of my head, but I can guarantee you Hemingway wrote bad sentences and published them. And there's also filler. I shouldn't say filler. There are also building blocks, sentences where, you know, "He grabbed a cup of coffee." You need that detail, but that's not exactly poetry. So, when one of these sentences does arrive in prose and you couldn't put "we all take a beating every day" in a poem—you'd go right over that. You wouldn't hang on to it, but in the context of this story, it's one of the themes. It's the theme.

Can there be a novel that opens up from one sentence, or even one where you came up with a sentence in your mind, and it evolved from that one sentence? You've never had that?

Oh, no, I've completely had it. I was laughing because sometimes the first sentence is so good that you don't need the novel, even though you do. "It was the best of times, it was the worst of times." Right? Yup. Okay. Next novel.

The beginning of a novel can be so profound, so inspiring, and so inclusive of everything that it just stops you short, and then you're like, "Oh my God, I have to keep going." But I would also argue there's the end line. Often with my novels and sometimes with my short stories, I have the end line. I have the finish line. I have the last sentence ready to go. And then I write toward it.

Can it also be, as you're coming up with the inspiration for a novel, it's the sentence that you know as a writer is the one true sentence. And even if it's tucked in the middle of chapter twenty-six and it's not bookending the novel, that to you is the black box of the novel?

This is a great interview because it's making me think of process, of things I've written. For *Reservation Blues*, my novel of so many years ago now, I had one line in my head and it was from a conversation I had with another student in writing class. He was a very religious person who was very sure about his ideas, and he was asking me what I think of God. I said, "God could be an armadillo, I don't know." I carried that sentence around for a couple of years. And I knew I needed it, but I didn't know why or how. Then when I was writing *Reservation Blues*, I realized in the middle of a theological monologue by one of the characters that ... "God could be an armadillo. I have no idea."

Where does it appear in the novel sequentially?

In the middle.

In the middle, but that was the first sentence, literally, that you wrote for that novel.

Yes, it was written in my head. It was hovering there. I knew it would be in there.

➤·◄

SHERMAN ALEXIE has earned the PEN/Faulkner Award for his short story collection *The Lone Ranger and Tonto Fistfight in Heaven* and the National Book Award for Young People's Literature for *The Absolutely True Diary of a Part-Time Indian*. He also wrote and coproduced *Smoke Signals,* which won both the Audience Award and the Filmmakers Trophy at the 1998 Sundance Film Festival. Alexie's more recent works include *Blasphemy: New and Selected Stories* and *You Don't Have to Say You Love Me: A Memoir.*

BORIS VEJDOVSKY

"Cat in the Rain"

What is your one true sentence and why?

You asked me to pick one sentence, and I cheated. I took two. It's in the first paragraph of "Cat in the Rain," and Hemingway is describing the war monument. It reads, "It was made of bronze and glistened in the rain. It was raining." So, what is glistening in the rain is the war monument that the characters can see from the hotel room. I like the extraordinary, modernist simplicity of the sentence. It could be the title of a poem by William Carlos Williams, like "The Young Housewife" or like Wallace Stevens's "Anecdote of the Jar" with this rhythmic repetition of words. The repetitions and the alterations are almost from a modernist poem. These two sentences form an image. They all of a sudden blur the rest of the world and all we're left with is this war monument and this off-season rain.

It doesn't seem like these Americans are observing that monument. It seems that they are too wrapped up in their drama to even appreciate the glistening of the monument and what it stands for, is that fair?

I think that's a great point because it brings us back to the question of the narrator. The most fascinating character is always the narrator whom you very often don't see at all, and you hardly notice because you take it for granted that words do come from somewhere. But we need to wonder who says that, right? Who says the monument glistens in the rain? And the same voice tells us that in the good weather people would come and look at the monument. But this is not in the good weather. There's a voice outside of the two characters that knows these things. Indeed, the two characters seem to be impervious. They would not know that artists came out and painted this scene in the better weather.

How does the war monument serve the story? Would "Cat in the Rain" be successful or completely logical if it started with the second paragraph?

You're exactly right. Those would be stripped away. It seems repetitive. So, what does that first paragraph give us? It gives us a moment in time, which is extraordinarily specific. This is a post-war moment. This is a post-traumatic moment like any war monument. The monument is there to commemorate publicly what a community wishes to remember. It's about remembering. It's about cultural loss. George on the bed is one of Hemingway's avatars of a veteran who's been too close to the war, who got his wings burned, to use a euphemism. It also tells us that they shouldn't be traveling there; they're evidently out of season and there's nothing to be done there. The opening of the story tells us that there are very few other tourists around; the place is basically deserted.

The paragraph also tells us that these Americans are perceiving this place because it says they're on the second floor, but this is the way Americans count floors. It's an American view of Europe. When I saw that hotel in Rapallo, I was offered by the man at the desk to go see the room. And, of course, I imme-diately realized I had been reading this wrong for the whole time, because it's on the European first floor, but it's an American second floor. Insignificant as this may seem, it changes the perspective on the monument and the whole construction of the scene.

It's after the war, it's a time when they shouldn't be there and you start wondering, "What are they doing there? What is the point?" There's this pointlessness of traveling to countries that tourists visit in the good weather and being there in the bad weather—and the very repetition of not just "rain" but "in the rain" and "cat in the rain" and "glistened in the rain" and the waves breaking "in the rain."

Do you view the "one true sentence" concept as more fruitful for examining Hemingway's early period?

It seems to me that it's more particular to his early periods, certainly whether it's through the conscious influence of people such as Pound or others is possible, but there's certainly an attention to rhythm, to the sound of sentences, very close to what you find in the poetry of that same period. There is also Hemingway's desire to use the simplest possible words. These are words a three-year-old child reads and understands. We say that every day, right? The weatherman on Channel Four says that every day, whether it's raining or not raining. We're not paying attention. It's almost phatic language and—like modernists in general—Hemingway takes phatic language out of its nonsense.

—

"So, all of a sudden, we realize how much is at stake
in the simplest possible statement."

—

So, all of a sudden, we realize how much is at stake in the simplest possible statement. That's one way I like to read Hemingway because otherwise one true sentence has a sort of magical aura, which I find much more difficult to deal with. What does that mean, one true sentence? True to what? True to whom? And if it isn't true, what does it mean? And if it isn't true, who do you betray? What is at stake ethically, aesthetically in that one true sentence? That's why I like sentences such as "It was raining," rather than sentences that would like to appear as simple, but are obviously symbolic and whatnot. What's at stake here is the difference between literature and the scriptures.

That is really interesting because Hemingway uses that adjective "true" in so many different contexts. I think it's worth asking if the word "true" always means the same thing to Hemingway or what the synonym would actually be. When I see something like "It was raining," your description of it suggests that it's really a brave sentence to write. It's really courageous and self-confident of a young writer to open himself up to that and in such a simplistic way.

Absolutely. Had I said that I would have said "simple"—you said "simplistic," but that's exactly how many people must have read that at the time. And some of my students do.

As you said, a three-year-old or a weatherman could say the same thing without being accused of being literary. "Cat in the Rain" is sandwiched in between interchapters of *In Our Time*, which seem like they're taking what you've been talking about, this conversation, and exponentially heightening the focus of the one true sentence.

Absolutely. And "true" is a very difficult adjective to deal with here. Even if you try answering those rhetorical questions in the way you just suggested: true to yourself, true to reality, you just fall on open knives of further rhetorical questions: What is your own self, or are you true to it? Do you know the real or what is authentic? It never ends.

It's interesting that Hemingway uses a very American word, "true." If you read Emerson, if you read Thoreau, you'll see that words such as "true" or "serious," which Hemingway uses quite often, are words that recur all the time. Thoreau defines a true writer as a serious writer. It's almost verbatim Hemingway.

➤·◄

BORIS VEJDOVKSY is Associate Professor of American Literature & American Studies at the University of Lausanne, Switzerland. His scholarship on "Homage to Switzerland" appears in *Reading Hemingway's* Winner Take Nothing. Among his works is *Hemingway: A Life in Pictures*.

MARK P. OTT

ONE TRUE SENTENCE FROM

"Big Two-Hearted River"

What is your one true sentence and why?

My one true sentence is from "Big Two-Hearted River": "The river was there."

I come to Hemingway through the lens of a teacher, and I always think of him as being so fundamental to how we teach close reading to our students. I think of that sentence like a brick in a Jenga tower. If you plucked that one out of "Big Two-Hearted River," if you plucked it out of *In Our Time* as a whole, if you plucked it out of Hemingway's whole accomplishment as a writer of fiction, I think thematically and ultimately didactically, what he's trying to teach us will be lost. So, it's really, in some ways, a distillation of so many of his fundamental ideas.

You have to keep in mind what would happen if Nick gets there and the river is not there. If it's polluted, if it's filled with garbage, if there are no fish in it. You think about how important it is to the sustaining structure of those short stories to find that clear, swiftly-moving water of that river. It's the same water we see in the first paragraph of *A Farewell to Arms*. It's the same water in many ways of the Gulf Stream that we see with Santiago. It's Hemingway looking at the life force in a way that is meant to show how essential it is to our spiritual rejuvenation, that once we have this deeper connection to the natural world, we understand our lives more fully.

Keep in mind that the story itself was begun in May 1924. It's right when Hemingway is becoming a father. It's not long after Hadley has lost the suitcase holding his manuscripts. He has to start over from scratch. And as he is doing that, this idea of the cycle of life, of becoming a young father, is so crucial to this shift.

He's contrasting the permanence of nature, in the case of the river, to the impermanence of nature in some of the surrounding aspects of the setting, isn't he?

Absolutely. And think about the word "there." That sense of a bedrock, something you can really rely on no matter where we are. That nature persists.

So, what about that? In the entire story, what does the Big Two-Hearted River mean for Nick?

It's so interesting to think about Nick's character development. We start with "Indian Camp" where we have the young Nick who is making a circle in the water that is like the circle of life. Then, of course, right before we get to "Big Two-Hearted River," we have "Out of Season," where the river is filled with trash. It's brown and muddy and beside a dump heap. "Big Two-Hearted River" is also placed right after "Cross-Country Snow," where there's this idea that he's going to get married. He's going to settle down. He's going to become a family man, because a baby is on the way. And in some ways there's that heart that belongs to his wife.

Then we get to "Big Two-Hearted River." There's no domesticity in that story. He's not in love with his wife and perhaps his emerging child; he's in love with nature. So, the heart is being pulled in two different directions at the end of the story. Keep in mind the last sentence: "There were plenty of days coming when he could fish the swamp," that beautiful ambiguity.

What is the swamp? Is the swamp going back and dealing with an emerging family? Is the swamp the mess of the divorce? Has he abandoned the family? Is this even the same character? Obviously, we have a certain sense of ambiguity here about the characterization that's meant to offer a broad range of interpretations, but the Big Two-Hearted River, that sense of being pulled in two directions, I think, is essential to Hemingway's characterization.

That's fascinating to bring up the swamp that ends up being the final note of the story. For Nick, is the river ultimately therapeutic, or are there hidden dangers within the peaceful façade?

Well, I think you have to see the river almost as a character, as something he has a relationship with. And like all relationships, you're going to have moments of joy and elation and good humor and fun. Catching a fish, a beautiful trout and bringing it on shore. Great fun. And then disappointment and perhaps betrayal. I think that's part of what Hemingway's trying to elucidate. Thematically it's a complete depiction of the natural world as a character in and of itself.

So much of what Hemingway does in his subsequent fiction is to circle back, to find some kind of meaning and connection to nature.

Did his relationship with nature or with the water evolve over time and over his career? Or was this always "the river was there"?

It's a tough question. And an interesting question. Look at the manuscript of *Islands in the Stream*. You see him seeking kind of that unity in a coherent form of a very ambitious novel that never gets fulfilled. Look at Thomas Hudson and his problems in that scene where he's drinking a lot. In that passage where he's driving to town and he says, "I drink against poverty, dirt, four-hundred-year-old dust." So, rather than having things that are rejuvenating, he's seeing garbage.

And conversely, going back to *For Whom the Bell Tolls*, where Robert Jordan is feeling life is leaving him: "He could feel his heart beating against the pine needle floor of the forest." He's deeply connected to nature. What makes *The Old Man and the Sea* work so well is that concision, but also the imagery. The dark water of the Gulf Stream is the greatest healer there is. It's this sense that water is going to heal us. And that Gulf Stream is part of the same river as up in Michigan, the same river in Spain. We get that deep connection. That's going to heal him in the same way that if you're in a good relationship with another human being, it's rejuvenating, it gives you the life force. Paradoxically, that's what you see at the end of living one's life.

—

"So much of what Hemingway does in his subsequent fiction is to circle back, to find some kind of meaning and connection to nature."

—

Really, you could take it from 1950 onwards where many of his personal relationships were not as authentic or as sustaining and mutual, that there was a certain transactional element to almost every relationship that he was in. People were feeding off his celebrity, feeding off of his money and his ambience. And that sequence from *Islands in the Stream* speaks to a period where something authentic is lost.

I love what you're saying about the river being a character and Nick and other Hemingway protagonists having relationships with the river. Santiago tests the limits of the Gulf Stream. When he goes out, he goes farther

than he usually goes. And Nick does the same thing. He wants to see how big a trout he can withstand and the depth of water he can withstand. So, he's actually doing something as a young man that Santiago would also do as an older man, to see what the bounds of nature actually are.

Well, I think it's interesting to know too, how that philosophy does pivot for Hemingway. When he first encounters the Gulf Stream, for example, in these rivers, the young Hemingway certainly is in the Teddy Roosevelt mold of somebody who wants to conquer and harvest nature. He wants to catch the fish. He wants to shoot the lions, partridges, and ducks. He wants to conquer nature.

But later in life, for Santiago and his fish, when he strikes the fish, "it was as though he himself were hit." Santiago is unified with the natural world in a way that a young Nick Adams catching that fish is still trying to understand his relationship with nature. Is he going to conquer it, or is he going to find some way to live in harmony or in peace with it?

➤·◄

MARK P. OTT is Head of School at Windsor School in the Bahamas. He is the co-editor of *Hemingway and Italy: Twenty-First Century Perspectives*, the author of *Sea of Change: Ernest Hemingway and the Gulf Stream*, and the co-editor of *Ernest Hemingway and the Geography of Memory*, as well as the General Editor for the Teaching Hemingway series with Kent State University Press.

MICHAEL MEWSHAW

ONE TRUE SENTENCE FROM

A Farewell to Arms

What is your one true sentence and why?

I think there's a world of choice, but what I've settled on is the opening of *A Farewell to Arms*, and I'm not going to limit myself to one sentence, because I think the rhythm of those opening sentences really is something to behold and to discuss. The opening sentences are: "In the late summer of that year we lived in a house in a village that looked across the river and the plain to the mountains. In the bed of the river there were pebbles and boulders, dry and white in the sun, and the water was clear and swiftly moving and blue in the channels. Troops went by the house and down the road and the dust they raised powdered the leaves of the trees. The trunks of the trees too were dusty and the leaves fell early that year..."

I could keep on going for several paragraphs. These sentences and this opening constitute for me what I believe Hemingway was talking about, about true sentences. I don't think he meant philosophically or philologically sentences that were true rather than false. There may have been some aspect of that, but I would like to concentrate on how in an architectural sense, these are true, in the way that a spirit level measures the truth of an architectural project. Their construction and the sort of architectonic aspect of the sentences suggest poetry to me.

Many people talk about Hemingway as being a realistic writer, but there have been any number of articles and books that actually emphasize the fact that his writing is anything but realistic. It creates a sense of realism, but the language is even today extraordinary. It's extraordinary in its composition, in the diction. It is something completely in and of itself. He's had many, many imitators and has had no end of influence on writers who followed him. But I think he, to an extraordinary extent, was able to master what he himself seems to have invented. I know that he gave some credit to Mark Twain and the American sort of vernacular and to Gertrude Stein. But the individual sentences are all his own. They're not all to everybody's tastes, but they're distinctively his own.

I'm fascinated to hear you refer to this as architecture. In *A Farewell to Arms*, Frederic Henry, of course, was in Italy to study architecture. I wonder if that is related to how the story itself is constructed. Are you saying that each sentence has to be true according to the work in which it appears?

That's an incredibly difficult protocol to follow for an entire novel. For a lyric poem, it's one thing; for a novel, it's another. But I think at his best, what Hemingway's aiming for is that kind of truth. I went last night and looked up the dictionary meaning of "true." And, of course, there was the sense of it's being "accurate" or "right" as opposed to being "false." But there's also talk of it being "something that's solidly built, accurate or exact, balanced, aligned, upright, level, appropriate, authentic." I think all of those things are better descriptors of what Hemingway was aiming for than the opposite of false.

I think it's possible to write a sentence that is completely false by any rational standard or by our common understanding, but nevertheless is beautifully constructed and effectively written.

Looking back at the projects you've written and that you continue to write, is Hemingway's one true sentence approach consistent with how you write?

In theory and ideally, yes. I think for a long time before I start writing, I at least try to get what a journalist would call a *lede*. And sometimes I try to have a conclusion before I start writing, but there is a way in which once you have a sentence or two that makes sense, or that seems appropriate, you can build on that, you can follow that with something else.

As you were honing your craft was Hemingway a touchstone?

He very much was, especially early in my writing so-called career. I mean, in high school and college and then in graduate school, I was very indebted to Hemingway and the structure of the sentences and the simplicity of the sentences and the understatement. Eventually I'm not sure that that very flat style worked for me. I think I may have been hiding any number of malfunctions on my part under that flatness, or the flatness that we speak of in Hemingway or the understatement in Hemingway has a resonance that mine didn't have. So, I tried in subsequent novels—after the first couple—to punch up the language a little bit and be more selective in my choice of words.

—

"His writing is anything but realistic.
It creates a sense of realism, but the language
is even today extraordinary. It's extraordinary
in its composition, in the diction."

—

You know, his influence is just so pervasive. There are, amusingly, people like Cormac McCarthy who have a very Rococo style, the external description and the external life of his characters is described in Faulknerian language. The inner life of his characters is very Hemingwayesque, very brief, specific, concrete.

Also, there's that thing which is important in Hemingway and became important to many other writers: that is that you don't name an emotion. You let the context of the scene and the language that's used lead the reader to say, "Ah, this is fear" or "This is loneliness" or "This is desire" or "This is regret or despair."

Very frequently it's misunderstood about understatement and the power of it. Understatement goes all the way back to Homer and the Greeks. It was called *litotes*, understatement for effect. And I read something recently that touched on this and it was by of all people the French writer Marguerite Duras, and she was talking about understatement and fragmentary, elliptical style. She called it a permeable style, as opposed to somebody like Balzac, who completely bricks up the space with descriptions and details, and doesn't allow the work to breathe. And Duras says that that doesn't allow any room for the reader, and that's one thing that is germane where Hemingway is concerned—the room that he provides for the reader to participate in the creation of his stories.

So, to take that point and then to apply it to the opening of *A Farewell to Arms*, what makes it powerful and suggestive rather than vague and overly broad?

Well, I suppose if you think of it pictorially, or in terms of a view, it's a close-up of a particular place. Then, by the second paragraph, we get down to him saying, "it was like summer lightning, but the nights were cool and there was not the feeling of a storm coming." You know, he's leading up to the description then of troops marching along this road. It's just the third paragraph and you're into it. And this opening paragraph takes on a kind of resonance. There's almost a biblical quality to this prose and to the repetition of words and the repetition of images and the repetition of sentence structure. If you read it out loud, it is to me as powerful as it is when you read it to yourself. Not all writers are like that. Not all of them are as powerful to be read aloud as they are when you're reading silently.

I would feel remiss if I didn't mention that, you know, this worked for Hemingway right up until it didn't work for Hemingway. And it's always debatable why it stopped working for him or whether the pressure he put on himself was such that he couldn't do it anymore.

><

MICHAEL MEWSHAW has published twenty-two books—eleven novels, four memoirs, two investigative reconstructions of murder cases, three books about professional tennis and two books of travel writing. He has won awards for his fiction, his investigative reporting, his tennis coverage and his travel writing. Hundreds of his articles and book reviews have appeared in journals such as *The New York Times, Playboy, Architectural Digest, Granta, European Travel & Life* and *The Sewanee Review.*

SEÁN HEMINGWAY

ONE TRUE SENTENCE FROM
The Old Man and the Sea

What is your one true sentence and why?

It's from *The Old Man and the Sea*: "A man can be destroyed but not defeated."
For me, it speaks to the resiliency of the human spirit. We've all got dealt different cards, but you can't entirely crush the human spirit. That line has general resonance, and it has even more resonance today. I think of how we all are facing this worldwide pandemic, COVID-19 and how we're all trying to get through this. We're all spending a lot of time by ourselves these days, and you get to know yourself and what you can and can't do, but the human spirit is an enduring thing. It is a great statement.

After working on the Hemingway Library Edition of *The Old Man and the Sea*, is there anything in the novella that has taken on a newfound significance that might have surprised you?

One of my other favorite parts of the book is when Santiago thinks about lions and his time off the coast of Africa. It is so interesting to think about people, solitary people, who have had great experiences and draw on their experiences from earlier in life. Santiago does that through dreaming. I found recently, sheltering at home, I've been doing mindfulness and the sessions involve traveling to places that I've been that have really meant a lot to me. It's very observant of Hemingway to bring that into the story. Hemingway brings in these elements of the story even though Santiago is by himself on the sea, or even in dialogue with a young boy. Santiago lives a very simple kind of existence, yet he's also had this rich life.

—

"We're all spending a lot of time by ourselves these days, and you get to know yourself and what you can and can't do, but the human spirit is an enduring thing."

—

And he draws on that as part of his strength. I think that's very true for many of us. Our lives change, but we have this rich well of experience. I think it's also a leitmotif for my grandfather. Think of *A Moveable Feast* when he returned to that seminal period of his youth in Paris at the end of his life. It's such a powerful time for him, and he remembers those experiences so vividly in that book. Memory plays an important part for us, whether it occurs in dreams or whether it occurs in daydreams.

Why do you think *The Old Man and the Sea* is so relevant these days? Perhaps not more so than other Hemingway works, but it seems like there's something timeless about it that maybe even *The Sun Also Rises* wouldn't quite have that same eternal quality. Is that fair?

I think it does have a timeless quality to it. It really has almost an epic feel to it. And the subject is approachable for many people. The notion of an individual having this sort of epic battle with a fish on the sea is perhaps more accessible to people than some of the other subjects of my grandfather, like those that are touched on in *The Sun Also Rises* like bullfighting or warfare. The language also makes it relevant. That's true of his work in general, but *The Old Man and the Sea* is a short book and his language is so approachable.

In your Introduction to *The Old Man and the Sea*, you talk about the ecological theme that's running through the narrative and Hemingway as a lover of nature and hunting and fishing. Does the ecological element to *The Old Man and the Sea* perhaps mean something different now than it did when he wrote it?

I think it does. As we see, the ecology of the world is in a state of collapse. People are talking about mass extinction and the number of animals and species that are going extinct. Even marlin are on our endangered species list. Marlin—which I read to my amazement at the Museum of Natural History in London a year ago—are the fastest fish in the sea. Quite amazing.

It's such a beautiful image that my grandfather portrays of the Gulf Stream and what it was like and how Santiago understands so much of it. Through the writing, we gain an appreciation for the sea and the Gulf Stream and get some understanding of this complex ecosystem and all the different kinds of creatures that are in it and how you can understand them and read the signs, in his case, to find the fish that he's looking for.

But there's also the balance of that, that these local fishermen are fishing on a smaller scale than fishing is happening today. I think one of the most remarkable images in this new edition is a photograph that I believe my grandfather took in 1955 around the time that they were making the movie for *The Old Man and the Sea*. It's actually two old fishermen with a marlin in their skiff. It's the same kind of boat as is described in *The Old Man and the Sea* and it's fishermen from Cojimar, the little village where Santiago fishes from. And there's the marlin. It's the size of the boat that's inside the boat, and there are two old guys with it.

It's just kind of amazing to see what these men were doing, that that kind of fishing was set up for catching such a fish and that the scale of it was within keeping of the ecosystem there. So, they weren't overfishing as is unfortunately being done around the world now. And the pollution also that's happening in the oceans is terrible. Then we have climate warming and that effect on fish around the world. This is a story that was written not that long ago, and we're really talking about how within many people's lifetimes these changes are happening. It's sad and can be seen as a call to action.

This may not relate to the environmental issues that you're talking about, but it strikes me as something similar. Hemingway ends the novella with the tourists and their obtuse dialogue. He must have been making some kind of a statement about outside intrusion onto some sort of holy experience that played out on a grander scale.

Yes. It is a kind of a great irony at the end. Almost like the ending of *The Sun Also Rises* with the last sentence. And again it's playing on not understanding. They don't even quite realize that it's a marlin that they're looking at. The kind of knowledge that's embodied in this book is remarkable in that it's so accessible to people. It gives people a window into what the sea is like. For many of us who are not sea people—I mean, I'm personally more of a freshwater fisherman, and I spent quite a bit of time in Greece on the sea—but when you read *The Old Man and the Sea* and you see all these signs of what for many people looking out at the sea just looks like this vast body of water, you can understand that it's home to this huge body of life. Hemingway gives you a vision of this remarkable ecosystem.

➤•◄

SEÁN HEMINGWAY is the John A. and Carole O. Moran Cura-
tor in Charge of the Department of Greek and Roman Art at the
Metropolitan Museum of Art, New York. A specialist in Greek and
Roman bronze sculpture and a classical archaeologist, he is the
author of numerous publications on ancient art as well as a novel,
The Tomb of Alexander. The grandson of Ernest Hemingway, he is
the editor of *Hemingway on Hunting* and *Hemingway on War,* the
Restored Edition of *A Moveable Feast,* and six other books of his
grandfather's writings, which comprise the popular Hemingway
Library Edition series.

HIDEO YANAGISAWA

Hemingway's letter to Charles Scribner

What is your one true sentence and why?

I chose this sentence, "[*The Old Man and the Sea*] is the prose that I have been working for all my life that should read easily and simply and seem short and yet have all the dimensions of the visible world and the world of a man's spirit."

That sentence is from Hemingway's October 1951 letter to his publisher Charles Scribner, right? Out of all of Hemingway's writing—fiction, non-fiction, and, in this case, letters—what is it about that one that struck you?

It explains the reason why Japanese readers like this story. This story expresses the human spirit as well as human reflections. For example, Santiago thinks about the reason why he was born to be a fisherman. The Japanese prefer those kinds of reflections.

What does Hemingway mean by "all the dimensions"? I ask that because Hemingway uses that key word—"dimension"—a lot when talking about his own writing. As early as the 1920s, he writes about how his work has dimension to it, or it should. He says it has three or even four dimensions.

Later on, he writes about how his work has five dimensions to it. For about thirty years, dimensionality seems important to his literary project. What do you think that phrase means here?

Well, Hemingway had been focusing on actual dimensions before *The Old Man and the Sea*. Then, in this work, he focuses on the human spirit, especially. He emphasizes the human spirit at the end of the sentence to Scribner.

When you say actual dimensions, it sounds to me like maybe you are talking about the third and fourth dimensions as space and time, these kinds of scientific, measurable units; or, in the case of Einstein, the way that modern science blew up the way that we think about how we can measure these things. Is that what you mean?

Yes, because in the former works Hemingway focuses on actual human pain that comes from something immediate, like war, or his mother, or things like that. In *The Old Man and the Sea*, he is focusing on the universal dimensions of time and age.

How was Hemingway inspired by Japanese and Chinese writers and historical figures, and where do you see that inspiration showing up in the novella?

As you probably know, he created this work based on anecdotes about Cuban fishermen. He decided to choose this real story, and I think he was wondering what type of character would be best for this story. During that time, Hemingway had the chance to read Japanese and Chinese books, actually. During the 1930s and 1940s, he needed to get a lot of materials to visit China as a correspondent. You can see a lot of books about China and Japan in Cuba, at his house. I actually found a lot of books about Japan relating to samurai spirit, and things like that. In *Hemingway in Cuba*, Norberto Fuentes wrote about an episode where one of the guests said that Hemingway often demonstrated committing suicide using a gun, saying this is the technique of hara-kiri.

—

"This story expresses the human spirit as well as human reflections."

—

Also, Hemingway admired a Japanese Admiral, Heihachiro Togo, who contributed to the Japanese victory in the Russia-Japanese War. Hemingway mentioned Heihachiro Togo in his introduction to *Men at War*. He started writing that introduction soon after Pearl Harbor. And still, he admired the way of fighting of Heihachiro Togo. While Hemingway, of course, criticized the Japanese way of fighting from the fair view of pure fighting, he admired the Japanese way of fighting in the Russia-Japanese War. That war can be seen as a structure of David and Goliath, and this structure can be seen in *The Old Man and the Sea*.

As a researcher, teacher, and board member of the Hemingway Society of Japan, you must have a good perspective on Hemingway's reception in the country. What is the current response to Hemingway and to a work like *The Old Man and the Sea*?

Hemingway himself is very popular here in Japan, and *The Old Man and the Sea* is special. That can be seen in the historical acceptance of the novella in Japan. For example, in 1955, the Japanese Ministry of Education selected *The Old Man and the Sea* as a special selection for educational films. Actually, my father remembered that he and his classmates got together in their school gymnasium to watch the Spencer Tracy movie. In the 1960s, *The Old Man and the Sea* appeared in the textbook for the course on Japanese language for public junior high school. Then, in 1999, the animation of the book won an award at the cultural festival hosted by the Japanese Ministry of Education. Now, at the moment, one of the biggest publishers in Japan has selected *The Old Man and the Sea* for a summer campaign every year since 1976. You can see the piles of copies in bookstores here and there in the summer in Japan.

There are obviously film adaptations of other Hemingway works. There are also other Hemingway works about protagonists on the water or individuals in tragic situations, or the idea of the indomitable human spirit. I do wonder what is it about that novella, especially, that speaks to the Japanese people?

In my opinion, there are three reasons. One is, as I mentioned, the beauty of a duel with the structure of David versus Goliath. The second is an admiration for the human spirit. This is the main theme of the story, right? The last reason is ontological reflections. Most Japanese can see that Santiago grows through ontological awakening, which is part of Asian samurais' life work. We Japanese focus on ontological awakening. That is one of the main reasons Japanese like Santiago's story.

>—•—<

HIDEO YANAGISAWA is Professor of Foreign Studies at Meijo University. He is the author of numerous publications on Ernest Hemingway in the Japanese and Chinese context.

PAM HOUSTON

Hemingway's letter to F. Scott Fitzgerald

What is your one true sentence and why?

My one true sentence is from Hemingway's letter to F. Scott Fitzgerald: "But when you get the damned hurt use it—don't cheat with it."

That's wonderful. What does that sentiment tell you about Hemingway?

It's something that resonates with me as a writing teacher. I've written a lot of books, but my real calling is as a writing teacher. The older I get, the more important it is to me to help get books out into the world by these younger writers. I can't think of the number of times I've said, "I have to see the blood on the wall," or something like that. One of my major roles as a teacher is to hold a space where a young writer can express the hurt and stay with it and write deeply and precisely enough into it that the reader is moved by it, changed by it, can have the experience of it. I think that's what Hemingway means here.

Hemingway was famous for all the ways he was hurt in his life. I guess most writers are. So what he's saying here quite clearly is: you can't gloss over it. You can't rush through it. I'm always saying in classes, "Stop protecting me from the bad thing that happened." I want to be in it. I want to be in that moment of the worst pain, not with a whole bunch of abstractions but with the actual physical details of the scene, even if it's emotional pain. I want to be deeply in the scene, and I want to stay in it long enough to feel the hurt.

One of the stereotypes of young writers, perhaps of the kind that would be in your class, would be people who wallow in their own pain. Are they avoiding that or are they just avoiding writing truly about it in the way that Hemingway instructs?

I learned from Hemingway as a young writer. *The Sun Also Rises*, for instance, was a book that was very important to me as a young writer. The main lesson from him was to sink the hurt and the pain down into the metaphor. The problem that you're talking about with some young writers is that they think filling up the pages with words like "hurt," "shame," "fear," "agony," "angst" is going to get the job done, is going to empty them of their soul full of emotions and express it to the reader. But it absolutely isn't. We need to see the dead deer on the side of the road, the dead pregnant doe with the warm babies still alive in its belly. Or your terrible grandfather who used to come into your bedroom at night. We need to see the saltshakers that he was turning on a lathe in the basement for hours while you were trying to get your homework done. You need to sink that pain into the physical world.

—

"You need to sink that pain into the physical world.
Hemingway was so good at that ..."

—

Hemingway was so good at that, and he taught me that if you fill up the pages with abstractions about your emotion, the reader may as well go outside and have a cigarette because you're doing all the work for them and you're not inviting them to participate in the scene that evokes those feelings. You have to ground the reader physically so that the reader can then bring their own emotions. You bring all your emotions and put it in the physical, and then the reader apprehends it in the physical and translates it back into their emotions. It's like a cable message being scrambled through the wires, and it comes out clear on the other side.

Well-chosen detail is an aspect of this.

Absolutely. I start there. I start in the physical world, not in the emotional world. My first job as a writer is to notice what I see in the world. I would not be surprised if this were true for Hemingway, but my first job as a writer is to pay strict attention when I'm out in the world. I collect things I call "glimmers," not because they're pretty, but because they vibrate, and those things, whatever they are, the grandfather's saltshakers, the dead deer on the side of the road, the color of the surface of a river late in the day when it turns into mercury, a woman backhanding her kid in the Walmart checkout line. You name it. It can be anything. I come home and I write those down and they become my raw materials as if I'm making really good soup out of organic vegetables.

So, I don't ever start with, "Oh, I have an emotion I want to express." I start with, "I have all these things from the world that lit up for me, that vibrated and said they were available to express some feeling I have inside," but I don't even worry about linking the feeling with the thing. I just look at my glimmers and say, "Okay, which of these glimmers feel hot? Which of these glimmers feel like they want to come out and play? Which of these glimmers feel like pushing on a bruise? Then, which ones feel like they want to interact with each other?" And the story kind of emerges out of the collaging of those glimmers.

When you accumulate those things that you're noticing, when do they suggest fiction to you or memoir or essay?

Yeah, it's a good question. I don't separate them literally on my computer. It's all just a big, massive pile of literally thousands of glimmers, but when I'm choosing them, often I don't know whether a thing is going to be called an essay or a story when I begin it. Often, I just bring the glimmers together and the story emerges slowly. If I have ten glimmers that happened on a trip to Mongolia, I know I'm writing an essay about Mongolia, but sometimes I really don't know. Sometimes I'm like, "Oh, fruit bats and orcas, and this ridiculous conversation I had in the Santa Fe Whole Foods parking lot. Let's see what that makes." Sometimes, I'm flying more blind than others, but often it's very late that I decide whether it's going to be called fiction or whether it's going to be called an essay.

Often that decision comes from how many liberties I've taken with the truth. I let the story direct me. If the story directs me far away from what has actually happened, even if it started with something that actually happened, then we're in the realm of fiction. Sometimes that can be fun. I was writing a story a couple of months ago, and I couldn't solve a problem. I thought it was an essay because it was about a trip that I recently took on the Green River. Then I suddenly realized the character had a sister and that made the story make sense—and I don't have a sister. I said, "Okay, I guess this isn't an essay anymore. It's a story," and then that really freed it up.

But sometimes the opposite thing happens. *Deep Creek* is my first book that couldn't have been fiction. All my other books could have been called either, and I would have been okay with it. We called most of them fiction because I strayed from the truth often enough that we decided they should be called fiction, even though they're all more or less autobiographical, but *Deep Creek* depended on being nonfiction. It had to be, and I learned so much about what it means to have to stay with what really happened and to wait for the meaning to emerge from it instead of blowing up a car, if you're bored, or inventing a sister, which you can do in fiction.

The quote you picked says: "don't cheat with it." Hemingway's not saying fiction is cheating and nonfiction is truth, right?

If you want to know about a genocide, for instance, read the fiction that was published about it rather than the nonfiction, because you're much more likely to get the truth. The great Barry Lopez was talking to an indigenous elder about the distinction we make between fiction and nonfiction, and the elder said, "That wouldn't really work for us." Lopez asked, "Why?" The elder said, "Well, we think about a story as an authentic story or an inauthentic story. An authentic story is about all the people and an inauthentic story is only about the writer himself."

PAM HOUSTON is the author of the memoir, *Deep Creek: Finding Hope In The High Country,* as well as two novels, *Contents May Have Shifted* and *Sight Hound,* two collections of short stories, *Cowboys Are My Weakness* and *Waltzing the Cat,* and a collection of essays, *A Little More About Me.*

MICHAEL KATAKIS

"Indian Camp"

What is your one true sentence and why?

My favorite of Hemingway's is from "Indian Camp," and it's the last sentence: "In the early morning on the lake sitting in the stern of the boat with his father rowing, he felt quite sure that he would never die."

Haven't we all felt that way in youth? We have felt exactly what that young man felt. You know you will die; but no, you don't. It seems so far away, perhaps something that you will never get to, even though you know you will. And, for a while, that feeling is intoxicating.

That feeling of immortality.

Yes, indeed.

Plus, it is a grown man, looking back at a childhood memory and incorporating a relationship with his father. And I'm thinking about how Hemingway captures youth, and fathers and sons in this narrative.

Yes. Look at this story. The young man's father is a doctor like Ernest's father. They loved fishing and being out in the wild. This is so autobiographical, and

Hemingway, even if this event did not happen, he can imagine it. He can imagine himself with his father and as a young lad asking this question, and then coming to that conclusion. I think Hemingway, throughout his life, is drawing upon everything that he's experiencing and seeing and hearing.

His comments about his advice about starting with one true sentence—which, by the way, works, and I use it—but where I found that it was equally helpful was applying it to the last line as well. So that you start with one true sentence, but you also end with it. And if it isn't true, to make it seem true.

When you write fiction, Michael, do you know what the last sentence is going to be when you start writing?

It's usually the first thing that's written. I don't know why, but I seem to be good at seeing the endings of things. It's the rest of it I find confounding, you know, getting to the end, but the endings are so much like a photograph. They are a snapshot of just a moment. And now you're trying to turn that snapshot into a full-length film.

When we talk to our guests about their one true sentences, it seems like a majority of them turn to these early stories. As you think about Hemingway, his career, and his prose, are you also drawn to the *In Our Time* stories as having some particular quality that, though great, perhaps later in his career was not quite the same?

That's a very good question. I can only answer it from my point of view. I agree with Edna O'Brien that some of these short stories are miracles. You look at them on the page and you just don't quite understand how they happened by human hand. They just seem to have always been there. The short stories for me are jewels and no matter what happened, I think they were so extraordinary that Hemingway had to measure up to the stories he had written in the beginning. Sometimes he got close, other times he did not. I happen to agree with Edna O'Brien about *The Old Man and the Sea*. It's lovely. It's terrific. But when I go back to the short stories, I'm struck by how amazing they are. And especially from a young man.

A story like "Indian Camp" that you isolated for today's conversation is also striking because as you read that last sentence, it sounds so beautiful and ideal. You kind of forget that, earlier in the story, there was unbelievable violence and trauma for this young boy. And I think one of the miracles that you're talking about is that those two extreme emotions can co-exist in just a few pages of this story. As a reader or a writer, how do you account for that kind of volatility in Hemingway's work?

The one thing that I have taken from "Professor Hemingway" is that to imply something is so much more powerful than explaining it all. Yes, we understand about the young man not being able to stand the screams of his wife, but he doesn't go into great detail of how the young man commits suicide. The mere fact that he does is so shocking, so horrific. Yet, you can understand if you identify with someone you love going through such horror, what it must be like. So, what I find so fascinating about Hemingway and so extraordinary is the implying of terrible, terrible things wrapped in such beautiful, beautiful language. You have almost like a Sebastião Salgado photograph of the workers in some horrible conditions for human beings, but the photographs are so stunningly beautiful that you almost feel guilty admiring, right? I love that kind of contradiction.

—

"What I find so fascinating about Hemingway and
so extraordinary is the implying of terrible, terrible
things wrapped in such beautiful, beautiful language....
I love that kind of contradiction.

—

I can see how you would view "Professor Hemingway" in your writing, but is there an equivalent in photography to implication and suggestion and not telling the whole story?

Absolutely. You've hit the nail on the head. One of the terrible things that has happened with digital photography is not the digital photography itself. It's the ability that one has now to pretend they are editor and photographer at the same time. In other words, there's no pause. So, you take many photographs when you should have taken one and then watch the world. When I'm asked to help young photographers, this is my advice. And I think it applies to the writing. You take your digital camera out into the street. You put in your mind how many rolls of film you have in your pocket. Is it one? Is it two? Is it three? Let's say it's one; you have thirty-six frames. That's all you get for the day. You take the photographs, and you never look at the screen until you are finished for the day and go back so that you are surprised by what you might have seen. I think this applies to writing. Don't keep looking back and forth. Let the characters speak to you. Let the reader be surprised.

Before the sentence you quoted at the end of "Indian Camp," there is an exchange between Nick and his father. That's all in dialogue and there are no speech tags. So, Hemingway's trusting the reader to hear the dialogue, the relationship developing between the father and son. Hemingway places a lot of trust in the reader, in this story and elsewhere. You're saying

photography works in a very similar way, with the relationship between the viewer of the photograph and the photographer?

Life is composing itself around you all the time. That is a fact of living. The question for me has always been, are you quiet enough and engaged enough to see it? I think what was happening with Hemingway was that he was seeing things as a young man and experiencing them. He was observing things like a hawk. He was looking at everything. Nothing escaped his eyes or his senses, the taste of food or drink, the way a woman walked. And he pared that down to the essential and he trusted that the reader was going along with him so that he didn't have to explain.

This discussion makes me think of the first couple pages of *Death in the Afternoon* where Hemingway is saying: "I was trying to write then and I found the greatest difficulty, aside from knowing truly what you really felt, rather than what you were supposed to feel, and had been taught to feel, was to put down what really happened in action; what the actual things were which produced the emotion that you experienced." That's obviously applicable when you would sit down to write as well as in photography. So, maybe not just one true sentence, but one true detail?

There's an irony I will tell you about photography. There is an irony. My photographs, before they reached the institutions they ended up in, I was very concerned all the time, very deliberative, paying very much attention, too much attention. It is when I started to absolutely not care about the taking of a picture anymore—was the aperture in the right place—that the pictures became alive. And I didn't know it at the time, but I made a conscious decision somehow, or an unconscious decision, to make a choice. The choice was to look at life and snap, and there might be imperfection in the photograph, but I would capture the essence of it. Hemingway is far more precise. Initially he is working with deep precision but making it look like it's serendipity. And that is the magic. And perhaps that is what's so elusive. Maybe that is at the heart of what talent is.

➤•◄

MICHAEL KATAKIS is a writer and photographer whose several books include the nonfiction *A Thousand Shards of Glass: There Is Another America* and *Ernest Hemingway: Artifacts From a Life*, which has been widely translated. His book of short stories is called *Dangerous Men*. He also served as an important voice in the recent documentary *Hemingway*, directed by Ken Burns and Lynn Novick.

NOTES

5   *He was about to take a drink, and he just said "blue gardens"*: The sentence from F. Scott Fitzgerald's *The Great Gatsby*, published in 1925, reads, "In his blue gardens men and girls came and went like moths among the whisperings and the champagne and the stars."

13   *Hemingway composed on the iceberg principle of suggestion or implication*: Hemingway's 1932 bullfighting treatise, *Death in the Afternoon*, contains his expression of this principle: "If a writer of prose knows enough about what he is writing about he may omit things that he knows and the reader, if the writer is writing truly enough, will have a feeling of those things as strongly as though the writer had stated them." Here, Hemingway elaborates more fully on that omission principle through the actual iceberg metaphor: "The dignity of movement of an ice-berg is due to only one-eighth of it being above water."

18   *He had all sorts of little superstitions*: In *A Moveable Feast*, Hemingway describes such superstitious behavior: "For luck you carried a horse chestnut and a rabbit's foot in your right pocket. The fur had been worn off the rabbit's foot long ago and the bones and the sinews were polished by wear."

20   *I read it immediately after hearing a Charlton Heston recording*: Heston's reading of Hemingway's 1952 novella *The Old Man and the Sea* was initially released through Caedmon Recordings in 1976, then in cassette recording through HarperCollins in 1992.

24   *Even though Hemingway supported the Loyalist effort*: During the Spanish Civil War, Hemingway aided the Loyalist, or Republican, effort in support of the

Second Spanish Republic, which was under attack by Fascist forces led by General Francisco Franco.

25   *Something that he saw in Stephen Crane's* The Red Badge of Courage: Throughout his 1895 novel about the U.S. Civil War, Crane refers to his main character Henry Fleming as "the youth." Hemingway reprinted the entire novel in *Men at War*.

26   *Considerably older than Hemingway was when Hemingway was in the war*: Hemingway was only eighteen when he enlisted in the American Red Cross.

26   *But he goes on and does the bridge mission anyway*: Working alongside guerilla forces in the mountains, Robert Jordan has been tasked with blowing up a bridge under Fascist control in order to help the greater Republican effort—a job that becomes a suicide mission.

27   *He gets eventually court-martialed*: During World War II, Hemingway violated the Geneva Conventions as a war correspondent by joining up with French Resistance fighters to protect the town of Rambouillet.

28   *It could be just a scream like with Henri Barbusse's* Under Fire: In his introduction to *Men at War*, Hemingway does call Barbusse's 1916 novel "the only good war book to come out during [World War I]."

29   *When the villagers are all forced over the cliff*: One of the characters, Pablo, forces Fascists to run a gauntlet (while villagers assault them with flails, pitchforks, and other weapons) that leads off the edge of a tall cliff.

31   *When he'd been tortured so severely after refusing to go home*: After his plane was shot down over Hanoi in October 1967, McCain spent more than five years as a POW in North Vietnam.

41   *He was wounded significantly during the war*: Hemingway was wounded by mortar explosion on July 8, 1918, while serving in the American Red Cross along the Piave River in the Veneto region of Italy.

42   *Poor Hadley, his wife, is beside herself about this new infatuation*: Hemingway and Hadley Richardson married in September 1921 and, a few months later, moved to Paris. Her concern about Hemingway's interest in Twysden would soon

be overshadowed by his infatuation with Pauline Pfeiffer, who would befriend Hadley in 1925 and become Hemingway's second wife in 1927.

43   *When I used to look at that famous photo of Hemingway*: This photo (with accession code EH05734P) is housed in the Hemingway audiovisual material at the JFK Presidential Library and Museum in Boston.

44   *There was a huge appetite for this kind of cult-of-youth modern literature*: Fitzgerald's novels and stories about youth include his 1920 debut novel, *This Side of Paradise*, about the life of Princeton student, Amory Blaine.

46   *You have Gertrude Stein, an American expat-in-Paris pioneer*: An experimental writer whose apartment (with partner Alice B. Toklas) at 27 rue de Fleurus was a favorite hangout of writers and artists, becoming a real space of influence on modernist culture.

46   *When he arrived in Paris, he was locked and loaded with letters of introduction*: Sherwood Anderson, the author of the important 1919 collection *Winesburg, Ohio* had met Hemingway in Chicago. Hemingway wanted to travel with Hadley back to Italy, but Anderson suggested the young writer go to Paris, and provided him with letters of introduction. Sylvia Beach owned the rental library and bookstore Shakespeare and Company, located on rue de l'Odéon, a short walk from Hemingway's small apartment on rue du Cardinal Lemoine.

48   *He's carrying all these memories with him and choosing to revisit Paris as a wellspring of sorts*: In late 1956, the Ritz Paris returned to Hemingway two trunks he had stored at the hotel since the 1920s. This discovery, or recovery, of material from his early Paris years became the genesis for writing *A Moveable Feast*.

49   *He's both exposing them and disguising them simultaneously*: When Hemingway arrived in Paris in December 1921, Anderson had supplied him with a letter of introduction to Stein. While in Paris he also met Fitzgerald and Ford. These three (along with numerous others) became the focus of individual chapters—such as "Miss Stein Instructs" and "Ford Madox Ford and the Devil's Disciple"—in *A Moveable Feast*.

50   *When Hemingway wrote about being up in Michigan, he was able to transplant himself*: In his chapter "A Good Café on the Place St.-Michel" from *A Moveable*

Feast, Hemingway writes, "I was writing about up in Michigan and since it was a wild, cold, blowing day it was that sort of day in the story. I had already seen the end of fall come through boyhood, youth and young manhood, and in one place you could write about it better than in another. That was called transplanting yourself …"

51   *I'm much closer to Hemingway or Martha:* The writer, activist, and icono-clast, Martha Gellhorn was Hemingway's third wife. They met in Key West in 1936, were married in 1940, and divorced in 1945.

51   *Picture Hemingway in his rooftop garret*: In *A Moveable Feast*, Hemingway reminisces in second-person about "the hotel where Verlaine had died where you had a room on the top floor where you worked."

54   *Is* In Our Time *something that Fitzgerald was likely to enjoy?*: Published in 1925, Hemingway's *In Our Time* weaves together short vignettes, or "interchap-ters" of World War I, bullfighting, and other violent scenes with longer short sto-ries, many of them like "Indian Camp" and "Big Two-Hearted River" that focus on Nick Adams.

55   *I've always thought of those chapters on Fitzgerald in* A Moveable Feast: These chapters include "Scott Fitzgerald," "Hawks Do Not Share," and "A Matter of Measurements."

56   *Agnes von Kurowsky jilted Hemingway*: After his wounding during World War I, Hemingway recuperated in Milan, where he met nurse Agnes von Kurowsky, who was more than seven years older than Hemingway. After he departed for the U.S., she wrote him a "Dear John" letter, telling him he was just a "boy," she a woman, and theirs more a mother-son relationship than true romance. Heming-way would write to his friend Bill Horne, "She doesn't love me Bill. She takes it all back […] I'm just smashed by it."

67   *Some of his audience would meet him halfway and know the story behind Tiger Flowers*: Less than one year after defeating Harry Greb and becoming the first African American middleweight boxing champion, Theodore "Tiger" Flowers lost the title to Mickey Walker—a.k.a. "The Toy Bulldog"—on the judges' deci-sion, a controversial result (in the eyes of ringside experts) that led to an investi-

gation. Flowers attempted to organize a rematch, but one never materialized, and in late 1927 he died from complications during eye surgery.

68   *Carlos Baker published in 1969*: The Hemingway biographer and scholar published these sketches in *Ernest Hemingway: A Life Story*.

68   *He had published, at this point, "A Divine Gesture"*: Published in *The Double Dealer* magazine, "A Divine Gesture" is a dreamlike and quasi-surrealistic story, complete with talking bathtubs and flowerpots.

68   *He had also written "Up in Michigan," but that's all he had*: One of Hemingway's earliest stories, "Up in Michigan" was initially published in *Three Stories & Ten Poems* in 1923.

69   *The kind of objective correlatives that he'll talk about in* Death in the Afternoon: In "Hamlet and His Problems," T.S. Eliot referred to the "objective correlative" as "a set of objects, a situation, a chain of events which shall be the formula of that *particular* emotion". In *Death in the Afternoon*, Hemingway would similarly investigate "what the actual things were which produced the emotion that you experienced."

70   *If you think about the beginning of "On the Quai at Smyrna"*: This story, published as the first story of the 1930 edition of *In Our Time*, is about a refugee evacuation during the Greco-Turkish War.

78   *He's trying to write a piece about Antonio Ordóñez*: Hemingway sought to chronicle the mano-a-mano between Ordóñez and Luis Miguel Dominguín (Ordóñez's brother-in-law) in *The Dangerous Summer*, which was serialized in 1960 and published posthumously in 1985.

81   *He said his dad had about as much in common with her as a coyote has with a white French poodle*: Here, Keach refers to excised material from the story "Fathers and Sons."

85   *Philip Young made that such an important cornerstone of Hemingway's scholarship*: Philip Young was a Hemingway scholar who wrote the influential *Ernest Hemingway* and *Ernest Hemingway: A Reconsideration*.

85   *Hemingway still had a pretty good relationship with his parents*: Hemingway's father, Clarence, would die by suicide in 1928, a tragic event that Hemingway would blame on his mother, Grace. Their relationship would become more strained over the coming years.

95   *And Nick's cross-examination of his dad is pretty good*: At one point in the conversation, Nick's line of questioning leads to confusion about what his father has heard vs. seen. Nick asks, "What were they [Prudence and Frank] doing?"
    "I didn't stay to find out."
    "Tell me what they were doing."
    "I don't know," his father said. "I just heard them threshing around."
    "How did you know it was them?"
    "I saw them."
    "I thought you said you didn't see them."
    "Oh, yes. I saw them."

109   *Michael Reynolds talked about that in one of his biographies*: Michael S. Reynolds was a Hemingway scholar who published, among other works, a magisterial five-volume biography from 1987-1999.

109   *This sort of repetition, similar to one we'll also see in "Soldier's Home," is conspicuous*: "Soldier's Home," published in *In Our Time*, also contains passages repeating what a character "liked" and "did not like."

109   *Horton Bay, Michigan, that's a small rural area*: Horton Bay is located in northern lower Michigan, near the Hemingway family's summer cottage on Walloon Lake.

110   *With stories like "Indian Camp" and "The End of Something"*: Like "Indian Camp," "The End of Something" explores the young protagonist Nick Adams's life. In the latter story, Nick breaks up with his girlfriend, Marjorie, while on a fishing trip.

113   *In* A Moveable Feast, *there's "hunger-thinking"*: Hemingway connects hunger to desire, creativity, and memory in the chapter "Hunger Was Good Discipline."

114   *Justin Rice at LitCharts has done some studies of Hemingway's prose*: In his "What Makes Hemingway Hemingway?" analysis, Rice examines sentence length, unique vocabulary, and quantity of dialogue, and demonstrates that not only were John Steinbeck's words and sentences often shorter than Hemingway's, but that Hemingway's sentences became longer later in his career.

121   *The other major description of the iceberg theory is in* The Paris Review: Published in spring 1958, Hemingway's interview contains the following reflections: "If it is any use to know it, I always try to write on the principle of the iceberg. [...] Anything you know you can eliminate and it only strengthens your iceberg."

122   *He didn't invent the cultural dictum of Ezra Pound's imagism that less is more*: Rule 2 of Pound's "A Retrospect," published in 1918, instructs the writer: "To use absolutely no word that does not contribute to the presentation."

132   *We know* In Our Time *has some words and phrases that have a British tone*: For example, the narrator of "On the Quai at Smyrna" uses conspicuously British vernacular—"My word yes a most pleasant business."

135   *According to a letter he wrote his parents from a hospital bed in Milan*: On August 4, 1918, less than a month after his wounding, Hemingway wrote, "The rainbow trout up in Hortons [sic] Bay can thank the Lord there is a war on. [...] Gee I wish I was up there fishing off the old dock."

136   *Paul Smith tells us that Hemingway was working*: Paul Smith was a Hemingway scholar whose works include *A Reader's Guide to the Short Stories of Ernest Hemingway* and the posthumously published *New Essays on Hemingway's Short Fiction*.

136   *It's important to note that before Ernest went to war*: Carl Edgar and Charles Hopkins were two friends of Hemingway from Kansas City. Edgar and Hemingway were friends from Horton Bay. Hopkins worked at the *Kansas City Star*. Both friends were immortalized in Hemingway's early works, "Big Two-Hearted River" (Hopkins) and "On Writing" (Edgar).

137   *He went this time with Bill Horne, Bill Smith, and Hopkins again*: Horne and Hemingway served in the Red Cross together and they would later room together

in Chicago. Smith and Hemingway were friends from Horton Bay. Horne and Smith would be members of Hemingway's wedding to Hadley, with Smith serving as best man.

138   *Hemingway even admitted in a letter that it was really a story where nothing happens*: This letter is to Gertrude Stein and Alice B. Toklas, dated August 15, 1924.

141   *As someone who's been trying to cultivate, for a few decades of my adult life, that Flannery O'Connor idea*: O'Connor wrote this statement in "The Nature and Aim of Fiction."

141   *John Gardner coined the phrase "psychic distance"*: Gardner describes this term in *The Art of Fiction*.

152   *The conceit of the play is that Hemingway's just found out Mary has left*: Hemingway's fourth wife, Mary Welsh Hemingway, with whom he was married from 1946 until his death in 1961.

154   *He had had plane crashes*: Hemingway and his wife Mary were involved in two plane crashes, just days apart, in Uganda in January 1954.

154   *Hotchner was one of my big go-tos for understanding who this man was*: A.E. Hotchner was Hemingway's longtime friend and the author of the controversial memoir, *Papa Hemingway*.

155   *He tried to run into the propeller of an airplane*: In April 1961, after Hemingway had left the Mayo Clinic, he attempted to shoot himself but was prevented. He returned to the Mayo Clinic, but during a plane refuel in Rapid City, SD, he tried to walk into the spinning propellers.

156   *His porch step on Kenilworth Avenue in Oak Park*: Hemingway's childhood home is located at 600 N. Kenilworth Avenue in Oak Park, IL, a western suburb of Chicago.

159   *John Dos Passos or somebody, did not slack to him*: Dos Passos was an American novelist and former friend of Hemingway known for his 1925 novel *Manhattan Transfer* and his epic *U.S.A.* trilogy, published between 1930-1936. Dos Passos

and Hemingway had a falling out during the Spanish Civil War after their mutual friend José Robles was murdered.

164   *Writing personal checks to the author*: Fitzgerald's fourth novel, *Tender Is the Night*, was published in 1934.

169   *It's Hemingway legend that he described Caporetto so perfectly*: The Battle of Caporetto took place in October and November of 1917 and resulted in a catastrophic loss for Italy against the Austro-Hungarian and German Armies, which included a humiliating retreat of some 90 miles to the Piave River.

171   *Italian morale was also eroded by the disciplinary regime instituted by General Luigi Cadorna*: General Luigi Cadorna was the Chief of Staff of the Italian Army before he was relieved in November 1917, following the debacle of Caporetto.

176   *"It was the best of times, it was the worst of times"*: The opening of Charles Dickens's 1859 novel, *A Tale of Two Cities*. In his notebook, Fitzgerald would refer—not to "The Short Happy Life of Francis Macomber"—but to *For Whom the Bell Tolls*, which he thought of poorer quality than *A Farewell to Arms*, as "Ernest's 'Tale of Two Cities' though the comparison isn't apt. I mean it is a thoroughly superficial book."

180   *When I saw that hotel in Rapallo*: Rapallo is on the Ligurian coast of Italy, about fifteen miles south of Genoa. Hemingway visited Pound in Rapallo, where the poet lived.

183   *Thoreau defines a true writer as a serious writer*: In *Walden*, published in 1854, there are numerous occurrences of "serious" or "seriously" associated with activities that are related to writing and reading.

185   *It's not long after Hadley has lost the suitcase holding his manuscripts*: In December 1922, Hadley was headed to meet Hemingway—who was on assignment in Switzerland—and wanted to surprise him by bringing a valise packed with most of his writing; however, she lost it, or it was stolen, at the Gare de Lyon train station.

186   *Look at Thomas Hudson and his problems in that scene where he's drinking a lot*: The sequence from *Islands in the Stream*, Hemingway's posthumous novel

published in 1970, reads: "I drink against poverty, dirt, four-hundred-year-old dust, the nose-snot of children, cracked palm fronds, roofs made from hammered tins, the shuffle of untreated syphilis, sewage in the old beds of brooks, lice on the bare necks of infested poultry, scale on the backs of old men's necks, the smell of old women, and the full-blast radio, he thought."

188   *The young Hemingway certainly is in the Teddy Roosevelt mold*: The young Hemingway idolized the hunter, cattle rancher, conservationist, and twenty-sixth president of the U.S., who, in his "The New Nationalism" speech from 1910, declared, "Conservation means development as much as it does protection. I recognize the right and duty of this generation to develop and use the natural resources of our land." Later, in his poem "Roosevelt" from his collection *Three Stories & Ten Poems*, Hemingway would acknowledge the profound influence of Roosevelt's "legends."

191   *I at least try to get what a journalist would call a* lede: An old newspaper term for the beginning of a story, it is spelled "lede" to distinguish it from the homonym "lead," as in the metal, which was used as a physical spacing material in the printing process when newspapers were still letterpress printed from hot metal type.

192   *It was by of all people the French writer Marguerite Duras*: Duras's many honors include the Academy Award for Best Screenplay for her 1959 *Hiroshima mon amour*. In a 1991 profile, the writer Leslie Garis asked Duras about her resistance to Balzac and other classical novelists. "Balzac describes everything, everything. It's exhaustive," Duras responded. "It's an inventory. His books are indigestible. There's no place for the reader."

190   *I know that he gave some credit to Mark Twain*: In *Green Hills of Africa*, Hemingway said, "All modern American literature comes from one book by Mark Twain called *Huckleberry Finn*."

200   *He needed to get a lot of materials to visit China as a correspondent*: During the early 1940s, Hemingway traveled to China with his third wife Martha Gellhorn and met with political leaders such as Madame Chiang Kai-Shek and Chou En-lai.

203   *My one true sentence is from Hemingway's letter to F. Scott Fitzgerald*: This letter is dated May 28, 1934.

209   *I agree with Edna O'Brien that some of these short stories are miracles*: O'Brien is a prolific Irish writer who was a central voice in the *Hemingway* documentary.

ACKNOWLEDGMENTS

Like the podcast that inspired it, this book was a team effort and benefited from the generosity of many, many friends and loved ones, both old and new. It is our honor to name some of them here.

First, we thank the good folks at Godine, our editor and co-conspirator, Joshua Bodwell, Celia Johnson, Brooke Koven, Tom Morgan, Joe McKendry, and the entire team for their vision, competence, and professionalism.

Thanks to the generosity and unstinting support of the Hemingway Society, its members and leadership. Specifically, Carl P. Eby, Kirk Curnutt, Suzanne del Gizzo, Gail Sinclair, Wayne Catan, and Cecil Ponder have been wonderful collaborators.

One True Podcast has benefited from the creative expertise of Susan Vandagriff and Julene Ewert, as well as the musical gifts of Thomas Josenhans and Dennis Malfatti.

Thanks to Matt Blank, David Davis, Robert K. Elder, and Mark Ott for their friendship and generous counsel. And to David Fox for the inspiration.

Thanks to Joe DePlasco, Michael McCormack, and Savannah Demande for their assistance before and after our interview with Ken Burns and Lynn Novick. Maya Franson graciously assisted our interview with Paula McLain.

We thank Michael Katakis and Stacey Chandler for their permission to use the image of Hemingway's *A Moveable Feast* manuscript from the John F. Kennedy Museum and Library in Boston.

We could not run our podcast successfully without the recording and distributing teams at SquadCast and Buzzsprout. We appreciate their help.

For their support, we thank Michelle Lehman, Lesley Pleasant, and Dean Ray Lutgring at the University of Evansville and Dean Chuck Lindsey and the Dept. of Language and Literature at Florida Gulf Coast University.

Our deep and eternal thanks to our families for putting up with the long hours, the ill-timed co-author communiqués, and the obsession over Hemingway minutiae. You bring meaning to our work. Always, love to Kristen, Luca, and Noah Cirino, and to Jordan, Wally, and Freddie Von Cannon.

One True Podcast—quite obviously—would never have existed and could not survive without our passionate, engaged listeners and our brilliant guests. We are so impossibly lucky to have that support. And we hope *One True Sentence* delights our readers, celebrates the ideas and perspectives of our guests, and welcomes newcomers to the life, work, and world of Ernest Hemingway. We present this book in that spirit.

ABOUT THE EDITORS

MARK CIRINO is the host of *One True Podcast*. He is the author/editor of seven previous books about Ernest Hemingway and serves as the general editor for Kent State University Press's Reading Hemingway series. He served as the literature consultant on the forthcoming cinematic adaptation of Hemingway's *Across the River and into the Trees*. Cirino teaches American literature at the University of Evansville.

MICHAEL VON CANNON is the producer of *One True Podcast*. He serves as an advisory editor on the multi-volume Hemingway Letters Project and is co-editor of the final volume of *The Letters of Ernest Hemingway: 1957-1961* (Cambridge University Press). He has published extensively on Hemingway's relationship with F. Scott Fitzgerald. Von Cannon teaches at Florida Gulf Coast University.

A NOTE ABOUT THE TYPE

One True Sentence has been set in Arno Pro Regular with Neue Kabel for display. Arno is named for the Italian river that flows through Florence and was designed by Robert Slimbach, one of the most prolific and influential designers of digital typefaces. Neue Kabel is a modern interpretation of the original type designed by Rudolf Koch in the 1920s.

Book Design by Brooke Koven